My Journey for
PEACE

To: Don
Thank you for
blessing me with your
presence. Child of the
stars. Peace & love

My Journey for PEACE

By

Hinton E. Harrison

Bookstand Publishing
www.BookstandPublishing.com

Published by
Bookstand Publishing
Gilroy, CA 95020
2069_16

ISBN 978-1-58909-370-6

Printed in the United States of America

DEDICATION

This book is dedicated to all the abandoned and abused children in the world.

Love and Peace
Hinton

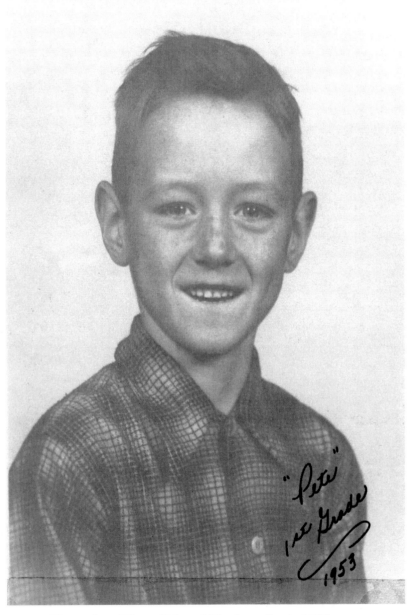

The author, Hinton Edward Harrison, Jr., in 1953.

FOREWORD

Hinton Harrison's wonderful new book, *My Journey for PEACE*, has a confessional prose style that reminds me of Jack Kerouac's books that I read when I was a college student in the fifties. Like Kerouac, Hinton journeyed alone around America and the world, trying to break free from society's strictures and find meaning to life.

His childhood was Dickensian. Shuttled between a variety of abusive stepmothers and fathers, he became a poster child for juvenile delinquency.

Ultimately, however, his spirit triumphed over his childhood adversity. As a young adult, finished with his military service in Vietnam, he led a nomadic life. He tried a variety of careers, most notably as a successful professional clown with the Ringling Bros. and Barnum & Bailey Circus.

Along the way, he discovered a latent talent as an artist. Today he is also a filmmaker, an author, a confidante, and a friend of many celebrities.

Joe Hyams
November 2006

Table of Contents

Table of Contents Cont.

Table of Contents Cont.

INTRODUCTION

Please allow me to introduce myself. I'm Hinton Harrison; and the book you're now holding is the first in a three-book trilogy, a puzzle of my life, that will guide you in better understanding my journey for peace and healing, my quest for innocence lost. I have been told that those who love you hurt you the most: When it becomes abuse there is no excuse.

In my life I have endured many nightmares, brought on by abuse both experienced and witnessed by me: Nights with no bedtime stories; nights when the Orphanage Monsters returned; nights and days of rage and whippings, so deeply painful; nights and days of being witness to the horrors of war. Through all my nightmares, however, the stars have always steered me through the darkness to safety. "Second star to the right, and then straight on till morning" lights the age of the "mind's true liberation."

My artistic style has evolved through the years, and is an expression of my childhood aspirations. My journey has taken me from my great grandmother's small farmyard in Claremont, Virginia, where I can remember, as a child, pressing my head against the screen on the kitchen door and looking up into the starry night sky, watching the stars twinkle.

I believe our very existence in its truest form is art, a miracle, and a unique creation. I am a child of the stars, a masterpiece, and a molecular phenomenon, formed into a human temple for the Holy Spirit in the physical world. I came to visit the Earth to be an emissary of love and peace. My purpose in this life is to be an artistic expression of the light within me. I find ways to express myself. My lighthearted nature is expressed in concepts that are produced in many mediums, spanning performing, filmmaking, photography, poetry, collages, and this book. Just being myself is an artistic expression.

My passion for expressing myself goes back as far as I can remember. It is my pre-encoded destiny to be an artistic visual expression of the light within me, sparked by a distant star. A brilliant connection that inspires me to radiate the joy I have for life. My erratic, unpredictable nature is always undergoing transformative change.

I use stars in all of my creations because for me the star means light, direction, guidance, and uplifting insight into creating visionary art. The star is associated with the energy and the clarity needed to actualize goals, as when you wish upon a star. The star is also a symbol of inner light that shines forth in the darkness. For example, the star is the symbol of Hollywood and all its glamour and success. Indeed, celebrities are called "stars."

I have always set my course by a spark of light that dwells deep within me and that shines brightly like the light of a star that shines on me. This light is my hope, and I trust my ability to survive. My guiding light gives me insight into the joy, the rapture, and the power that have no external trappings. When I express my visions, I give birth to creation.

I am always fascinated by how people respond to the images I create. It is a way of understanding the human psyche and human nature. For me it is a therapeutic process, and could be considered as revolutionary. The significance of my observations is expressed in my art. My art is an expression of who I am, and through my art I express my appreciation for life. And if I can inspire just one person, this is my priceless reward.

Through the face of peace, through the light of the many years, we have traveled in trust with the Great Mystery that lives within all. Peace Star Children, our innermost Mystic Being reveals the wisdom of loving kindness. From Omega Point to now riding the cosmic waves of light, a quantum molecular phenomenon.

We are each a living vision, dancing, singing, peace in the heart, peace in the mind, peace in the eyes, peace in every breath and heartbeat. Inspiring the truth of the Creator's dream on this precious place we call Planet Earth, our home, our mother of all life.

Here is a quote by T. H. Huxley that I would like everyone to think about: "Sit down before fact as a little child, be prepared to give up every preconceived notion, follow humbly wherever and to whatever abyss nature leads or you shall learn nothing."

I have always loved unconditionally. If my love has been overwhelming at times, please understand that my passion for life is the precious gift of your friendship. With deep warm-hearted gratitude, I wish to thank you for blessing me with your presence.

I Love You, Always,
Hinton (Pete) Harrison, July 2007

(Photo by Marco Franchina.)

The author, Hinton Edward Harrison, Jr., today.

CHAPTER ONE
HARMONIC CONVERGENCE, WORLD PEACE, ROSWELL, AND ME

The Commonwealth of Virginia birth certificate of vital record states that Hinton Edward Harrison, Jr., came into birth at the De Paul Hospital in Norfolk, Virginia, on January 4, 1947, at 11:49 a.m. Nineteen forty-seven was also the year of a harmonic convergence that ushered in World Peace, as well as the year in which Nicholas Roerich, who created the Banner of Peace, passed away, and in which the Roswell Landing in New Mexico helped trigger the UFO phenomenon. The child was born to Hinton Edward Harrison, Sr., and Malvine Marie Murphy, and their place of residence was Virginia Beach, Princess Anne County, Virginia.

This book is my life. It is not a bedtime story, but more like a jigsaw puzzle in a box. All the pieces to the picture are mixed up, and you have to dump them on the floor and then assemble them all to form in your mind a picture of my life and me. My life may also be looked at as a comedy of errors — or, in some ways, as a comedy of terrors.

On September 12, 1999, my Dad, Hinton Edward Harrison, Sr., passed away after years of suffering from crippling health problems that physically wore him down. At his funeral I decided it was time to find my mother, Malvine Marie Murphy, whom I had never met; it now seemed more important to do so than in the past. She had left when I was 17 months old, and I felt it was time to make this completion in my life now that Dad was no longer around. I felt the urgent need for closure with her; it seemed like the right thing to do. If she passed away before I could meet her, I would always regret having not at least tried to contact her. Most of all, it was important for me to meet her because it would force her to acknowledge my existence after denying it, after denying me, my entire life. Coming face to face with her would be enough for me.

1

I found out that my mother lived in Florida, was married, and had three daughters. That meant I had three more sisters and was the only boy out of six children. My mother had six children, of whom she abandoned three and kept three. A few years earlier, while passing through Virginia and checking out the Edgar Cayce Center, my psychic insights were working; a fun game to play is rock, paper and scissors, a psychic (in.tu.it) exercise. While there, I decided to drop in and see my maternal grandmother, who just happened to still live in Virginia Beach, to acquaint myself with her. It was a brief visit, our first meeting since my birth, and she gave me my mother's phone number and address. My first contact with my mother was by a letter I sent to the office where she worked. She called me and was really upset. I thought this was a funny or, should I say, bizarre response. She told me not to send letters to her at work; she didn't want her coworkers thinking she was having an affair. Yeah, right! You could just see the headline: "Mother and Son Get Back Together After 50 Years of Separation and have SEX." The Oedipus complex, as it were. I then placed a call to her home phone. She answered and I said, "This is your long-lost son." There was a moment of silence. Then she said, "Why are you calling me now? I am happily married and my husband and family know nothing about you. Please don't upset my life."

I told her that Dad had passed away and that I wouldn't be happy until I saw her. She responded by saying she would not meet with me, but I told her I knew where she lived, and asked her if she wanted me to come knocking on her door. She hung up at that point. Later my phone rang and it was her brother, my uncle, Murphy, threatening to kick my ass if I didn't stop bugging her. I told him to chill out and that it was time my mother acknowledged my existence. This was my first contact with Uncle Murphy, whom I had never met or spoken to before. I told him that I wanted nothing from my mother except to meet her before she passed away — or before I passed away first. I said that the sooner we made this meeting happen, the happier we would all be, and then I would go on my way and leave everyone alone.

He said he would get back to me, which happened while I was on a trip, driving through Donner Pass, California, on my way to San Francisco. (You've heard of the Donner Party, the pioneers who became stranded and had to resort to cannibalism to survive after running out of food.) Anyway, he called me back and said my mother would see me under certain conditions. They were that I could not ask about the past, and that there would be no blaming, no touching, and no crying. If I agreed, she would meet with me at a location not near her home. This was fine with me; of course, I would have agreed to anything to make this meeting happen. This reminds me of the movie *AI Artificial Intelligence*, which was about what it's like to be abandoned. Steven Spielberg did a great job on this story; he had his finger on the pulse of the issue of a child (in this case, a robot child) just wanting his mother to acknowledge his existence, to say, "I love you son."

The audience response to AI was that the child wasn't real; it is unimaginable that a parent could feel that way about their real, human child. Another film, *Bambi*, Disney's animated feature giving human feelings to animals, was an emotionally moving story about being left alone. It was all about separation from the mother; this theme in the film's story triggered some deep feelings in me. Walt Disney was a kind and loving person; you could sense this in his stories, in the characters he created, and in his demeanor. When I watched him on television when I was a kid, Walt showed a kind, sweet, gentle side I could only wish upon a star for Dad to have had. Another film that hit home to me was *The Elephant Man*, with Anne Bancroft, my favorite female actress, and with John Hurt as the Elephant Man. The abuse was heart wrenching in films of this sort, always bringing up emotional wounds tied to my own physical and mental abuse.

Returning to *AI Artificial Intelligence*, if I could I would ask the film's character Mr. Know the following: Are human beings the key to existence, the proof of genius? I would also tell Mr. Know of my wish to be taken to that place where dreams are born, where there is PEACE.

I don't go to horror movies. Some people love these kinds of films, but it has to be because they have never seen or experienced abuse in real life. They think it's just a movie, just entertainment. But if you have ever actually experienced physical violence, or seen such violence inflicted on someone else, it is very hard to watch on the screen. Personally, I have no desire to sit through this kind violence, so I just don't go to see these types of movies.

Returning to my story, Uncle Murphy called me back to tell me when and where the meeting with my mother would take place — Pointe Vedra Beach, Florida, south of Jacksonville; and he made it clear that the meeting would be brief. This sounded like a rude reminder to me that if I did anything to hurt his sister, he would kick my ass. I laughed to myself, thinking what a hell of thing it was to have to go through all of this just to get my mother to acknowledge that I existed.

I called an airline and booked myself on a flight to Jacksonville, with a stopover in Atlanta, Georgia. I purchased the ticket with $500 that my stepmother, Rose, had given me, the money that Dad had on his person when he passed away; she had told me that the money was my "inheritance."

The wisdom that I have learned from my relationship with my parents and other relatives, from my life experiences, and from witnessing human dynamics, has taught me that people can be mean and spiteful. The lessons I have learned, although often hard and cruel, have been valuable; have made me who I am. I have learned to have a keen sense of awareness. Believe me; I can sense danger when in a person's presence just by their

4

behavior, their body language, and their tone of voice. You can look a person in the eye and tell whether or not that person is a kind, loving, compassionate human being.

At the Atlanta stopover during my flight to Florida, on January 21, 2000, I learned that there had been a big snowstorm the night before, stranding passengers at the airport. While walking to my gate to make my connection, it was announced over the public address system that if anyone would give up their seat and catch a later flight, they would be given a voucher that was good for a ticket to anywhere in the world. I immediately went to the ticket agent and offered my seat.

I did this because, in the back of my mind, I had another wish: To go to Ireland, something that had always been a dream of mine. Thinking that I could use the voucher to travel there one day, I accepted it and stuck it in my pocket, then waited for the next flight. Time passed quickly and before I knew it, I was on my way. Arriving in Jacksonville late that evening, I booked into a motel, where I spent a restless night in bed, thoughts racing through my mind. A few years earlier, I had experienced a dream that stirred my desire to find my mother. In my dream, the inner child in me awoke crying out for its mommy, giving me the realization that the time had come for me to find her. I had been rehearsing exactly what I wanted to say to her from the moment I decided to make our meeting happen.

The next morning I arose early, freshened up, and caught a bus to the meeting site, Pointe Vedra Beach, south of Jacksonville. Boarding the bus, I told the driver drop me off at McDonald's, the place my mother had chosen to meet me. Presently the bus stopped and the driver said, "This is your stop." Exiting the bus, I crossed the street and entered the McDonald's. Inside I looked around at every woman who could have been 73, my mother's age, wondering if this or that woman was my mother. No one seemed to be looking for me, so I sat down in a booth and waited, watching everyone who walked through the door. Suddenly a woman accompanied by a tall, elderly man walked in and looked around. Seeing me, they walked towards my booth. Reaching me first, the man said, "I am a sheriff. I will be keeping an eye on you." He noticed my camera and added, "Don't take any pictures."

CHAPTER TWO
I MEET MY MOTHER

My mother sat down across from me. The sheriff, a friend of hers, sat down next to her with his arms crossed, staring at me with menacing eyes. The first thing I did was to set my camera on the table, secretly taking a picture by pushing the shutter button as I set the camera down. I looked at my mother for the first time since I was 17 months old. She began the conversation by saying, "Your father left me." This was neither Dad's story nor what his side of the family had always told me. What they had told me was that my mother had walked out, leaving me in my crib, unattended, never to return. Nor, they also had said, had she shown up in court for the custody hearing. There are always three sides to the story: The truth, Dad's story, and my mother's story. But the reality of the situation seems to be that neither Dad nor my mother was a responsible parent; they had both been young and wild.

They had met in 1945 after World War Two, when the country was celebrating in a new spirit of freedom and independence that fired up the hearts and minds of a new generation. The beginning of the American Dream was the buzz. Taking a deep breath, I looked my mother straight in the eye. "I just want to thank you for giving me life and this opportunity to tell you I love you. That's all I have to say," came my words. We gazed at each other, warmth filling me. My heart felt like it had found what it had been longing for all my life. Although they say searching for happiness is what makes us unhappy, was this going to change anything? Who knows? If I had been a cute little boy, she probably would have scooped me up in her arms, hugged me, and kissed me all over.

Then she told me she didn't have a whole lot of time, as she had to get back to her husband, who was sick in bed.

We had lunch, during which I sensed that she had issues. She told me how much I looked like Dad; I'm not sure if this was good or bad. She talked about my grandfather, revealing that he was not a likable person. He had never had anything good to say about her, either. Perhaps this was understandable. My grandfather was a tough old goat, living in the country, living in a time, in which you had to be strong in order to survive. His country ways were simple, and he did not like the fancy ways of the city folks. He had told me that my mother had walked out, leaving my half-sister by her previous marriage, Martha Gayle, before she had left Dad, leaving both Martha and I alone, never to return. Martha had spent more time with our mother than I had, seven years, and had thus formed a closer bond with her than I had. For Martha, therefore, her separation from our mother was even tougher than mine, and Martha had some serious anger issues as a result.

I told my mother of my desire to visit Ireland, and asked her if she had ever been there. She said she had, and that she had family there. I asked if she could give me some names of relatives there, but she smirked and said "No." I explained that I just wanted to get in touch with them, in touch with my Irish heritage. After lunch, we walked into a gift shop where I bought a little crystal dolphin that caught my eye. It would be a treasure, a memento, of my meeting with my mother, a reunion for which I had so deeply longed all of my life. My choice of the crystal dolphin held a special significance: Once I'd had a dream about dolphins in which they had telepathically called to me, and an intuitive instinct led me to swim with them. Their sonar echo pulses, their songs, had unlocked a deep primordial awareness in me to be like a child and set myself free.

As we walked to my mother's car, I stepped next to her and put my arm around her shoulder. She seemed uncomfortable with this gesture, saying, "I don't know you."

The saddest day of the year for me is Mother's Day. I often find myself staring at a mother and child, touched by that loving bond which is so important. It has always been hard for me to sincerely love my stepmother, Rose, about whom I write much more in later chapters. Here, it is sufficient to reveal that my stepmother, to say the least, was neither loving nor affectionate, and we had no relationship to speak of. And now, after never having had a relationship with my real mother either, she had just told me that she didn't know me — meaning, in effect, that she could not be my mother. Nevertheless, I still felt a telepathic calling between us, so I just responded by thanking her for showing up. Meeting her at last meant a lot to me, and I was finally satisfied.

As she drove away, I found it hard to believe that I had finally met my mother. I hoped that now, at last, my wounded inner child would be free; no more tears for mommy. I spent the rest of the day at the beach fishing, thinking about the good times Dad and I had enjoyed fishing together. One thing Dad had loved to do was fish and, believe me; we caught our share of fish. I have probably eaten every kind of fish that can be eaten, my favorite being salmon, although when I was a kid I liked catfish and hush puppies.

CHAPTER THREE
THE EMERALD ISLE

A year later, on January 18, 2001, I was on my way to Ireland to, I hoped, find and connect with my roots. I flew into London and hooked up with a friend named Chimpy, who had a van, and we traveled through the countryside.

Stonehenge, a sacred ancient distant place of curiosity and fascination, is now a part of my being. I went to the British Isles in search of spiritual purpose. As I wandered around, I marveled at the great, astonishing, mystifying architectural engineering feats resulting from human eco-cooperation. Stonehenge is still a gathering place where people come to study the past, where my ancestors pondered their relationship with Heaven and Earth — a center with correlations to the sun and its solar system.

My next stop was the Barge Inn, a charming pub along the Kennet and Avon Canal, one of the meeting places for crop circle enthusiasts. It is an area in which many crop circles have materialized, in geometric patterns, and I was there to get a feel for the phenomenon. There are many hoaxes and forgeries inspired by genuine crop circles; some are man-made. Crop circles are referred to as *Agrighs*, and they mimic atomic structure. How fascinating are the unknown forces, the universal matter that creates sacred geometry. All forms of life are born out of the center of atomic structure, a harmonic resonator of sound frequencies producing sacred geometry, the building blocks of life.

What this is all about is sound, the diatonic ratios of the music scale, so basically sacred geometry is "frozen music" comparable to a snowflake pattern; no two sacred geometry sites are ever alike. Sound vibrations and frequencies create geometric shapes, allowing us to witness frozen music. They are like keys unlocking cellular memories, awakening consciousness. Those who have their antennae extended and are receptive may find that they have the capacity to transform the planet, making it a better place in which to live in just by using a sound ("OM"). For further information on crop circles, I suggest you check out the Crop Circle Connector website: www.cropcircleconnector.com.

I also visited Glastonbury, and for some reason, upon my arrival, I thought about Sedona, Arizona; both places have a similar spiritual atmosphere. Of great interest to me was the Chalice Well, a timeless sacred place of birthing of the deepest, most magical dreams, where peace and love for the Earth and its inhabitants abound. It is a gentle place, where the soul is lifted and the veil between the physical existence and the Great Spirit disappears into the "Love Chakra." A feeling of universal intelligence, a pure radiant beauty, suffused my being with light as I drank the life-giving elixir of Mother Earth (Gaia) from the Chalice Well. It filled my holy grail of being with love and compassion, and deep peace and inner joy overcame me.

After a fun adventure with my friend Chimpy in England, I took a Ferry from Holyhead, Wales, across the Irish Sea to Dublin, Ireland. This is a wonderful way to travel because you meet very interesting people from all over the world; there was something special about crossing the Irish Sea. When you arrive, you walk off the ferry right into the streets of Dublin. The first thing I did upon disembarking was to find a Youth Hostel. Checking in, I started meeting other travelers. There were lots of treasures to be discovered, including the National Museum of Ireland, a great place to start in appreciating the history of this magical land.

Ireland has made a rich literary contribution to the world. I had fun visiting the Trinity College Library, where the *Book of Kells* is stored, and the Dublin Writers Museum. I was inspired being in the homeland such names as Shaw, Yeats, Joyce, Beckett, and Wilde. This, alone, was worth the whole trip.

The Tara, a sacred place possessing strong life force energy, also captivated me. Dating back to 2,500 B.C., the Tara is an upright stone — very phallic-like — standing in the middle of a mound from which you can see the horizon in all directions with a sense of clarity. It is a place of coronation, where my Crown Chakra lit up like an emerald. The Tara is called the *Lia Fail*, "The Stone of Destiny," and destiny is what my journey there was all about. It is a mythological place, the womb of Mother Earth, and the reason I was there was my mother. This place is called Goddess Maeve, the entryway to the otherworld, to a life of eternal joy and plenty surrounded by pure, clear, flowing, healing water. Soon, orienting my inner gyrocompass to this longitude and latitude, I felt connected with my Irish roots, felt a sense of place and birth. I felt great prospects here.

I ended my journey at the sacred passage tomb at Newgrange, located near the town of Slane, northwest of Dublin. The entrance of Newgrange is marked by a decorative stone. Three spirals there reminded me of the three stars in Orion's Belt, called the Three Stones of Creation by the Maya and many other indigenous peoples around the world. Entering, I proceeded down a long stone passage. Reaching a shamrock-like chamber, I stopped and stood in the chamber's center. The guide turned the lights out and, for a moment, the darkness was pitch black. Installed in the chamber is a light effect that simulates the dawn light as it appears on the morning of the winter solstice, the shortest day of the year, December 21st.

As I stood there, the shaft passage was penetrated by the simulated beam of dawn light, which crept slowly to the very back of the chamber, dramatically illuminating the chamber, recreating the key moment in the solar calendar. At this serendipitous moment, my soul awakened and the dream in which I had been living suddenly released me, wonderful thoughts entering my mind. The very same thing must have happened to the Neolithic people, the original inhabitants of this land, who had built this place more than 5,000 years ago in order to capture and experience this very moment each year, standing in the very spot I was occupying. I realized that everything between me and my source star is the brilliance of my gift of being. I always feel enthusiasm for the earthly experiences, such as this, that we share. What a wonderful gift life is.

After arriving back in Aspen, Colorado, where I lived during this period, I heard that there was going to be a gathering at Harris Hall to share condolences over the death of Rick Buesch, the local veterans leader, who had recently taken his own life. Again I am reminded of how precious and fragile life really is. We hang onto this invisible thread, hoping the strength to live never leaves us. Rick's death came as a shock because he showed me courage and strength that moved me out of shame and denial into honor and commitment for my brothers who had served so bravely, some of whom had given their lives, in the Vietnam War, a senseless war.

After some introspective soul searching, I'm still at loss over Rick's death. I expressed my feelings about this to a friend, who gave me the following words from David Wilcox:

> You're so strong and that's your crutch/To keep alone and out of touch/To try to keep your heart from the line of fire/So it's still trapped inside that war/Like there's a soldier at the door/It's time you told that soldier to retire/And bring 'em home/Bring 'em home/Both the mighty soldier and the boy.

There is a banging, banging on the door, a terrified, screaming, and a boy struggling to free himself. Someone please open the door. Never mind, it's OK. The door to Heaven is always open. You need not be concerned; the child has been embraced in the loving arms of the Creator of Love and Compassion for all. Home at last, home at last. Veteran brother Rick, Rest in Peace.

CHAPTER FOUR
NAM

As I said at the beginning, my life is like a jigsaw puzzle you dump on the floor and begin assembling, piece by piece. The picture that appears is a very surrealistic image. It is interesting how the human psyche works. As I tell you my story, it triggers in my mind images of yet another war we have gotten into, sending our young men and women, our children, off to a distant foreign land to die for . . . What?

Jumping back in time, the summer of 1967 saw the Vietnam War draining America of its poor youth. The draft was a lottery, and my number was called. I was 19 years old, living in a blue-collar, working-class, factory neighborhood. My draft notice appeared in the mailbox, stating "You are hereby directed to present yourself for Armed Forces Examination by reporting to the local draft board."

After passing the induction physical examination, I was sworn in with about 100 other young guys, all of us crowded inside a single room. The person about to swear us in divided us into two groups; one group would go into the Marines and the other into the Army. I took one step over the Army-side line, as I didn't see myself as a Marine. Before I knew it, I was stepping off a bus at Fort Bragg, North Carolina, at about 3:00 o'clock in the morning, where I was greeted by a drill sergeant's yelling.

"This is your new home and I am going to make a man out of you!" he shouted. "I am not your mother, your father, your sister, your brother, and for damn sure not your girlfriend! Now fall in line!" I am not going to go into the details of my basic training experience at this point. I have some interesting stories about it, but they aren't what I want to tell you about right now. What I will tell you is that it's tough making it through basic training, no matter what branch of the service you're in; and you really have to be mentally and physically tough to make it through the ordeal. Nothing, however, prepares you for actual combat.

I want to share with you something that popped into my mind after reading a *Los Angeles Times* article about a Vietnam veteran who flipped out back in the 1970s after returning home from Vietnam. He had held some people hostage in a park, demanding to see a psychologist. After the psychologist talked him into freeing the hostages, the veteran was interviewed by the press. He revealed that he had been a sniper in the military, that he had killed more than 300 people, and that he was pleading for help. This, for me, brought back a memory.

In 1968 I was in Dong Dam in the Mekong Delta with Troop D, 3rd Squadron, 5th Cavalry, 9th Infantry Division, in a flight control briefing room before being sent out on a mission. The commander pointed to an achievement list of soldiers who were receiving merits for the number of kills they had made, by unit; and he brought to my attention the fact that my name was not on the list.

I responded by informing him that my name would never be on the list, and that I refused to participate in any "competition" to kill as many people as possible.

I came to this realization, to this position, as a result of the events of our mission the previous day. Flying just below treetop level in our Huey UH-1 helicopter, we were patrolling one of the river tributaries on the Mekong Delta. I was manning one of the chopper's machine guns. Suddenly we came upon a sampan in the water, carrying an old man and old woman, both of whom were wearing civilian clothing.

The pilot hovered the chopper over them, and I could see that their hands were raised and that the woman was waving a small South Vietnam flag. By all appearances, this wasn't in any way a threatening situation. Nevertheless the pilot barked the order, "Shoot them!" And, in that instant, I found myself in an extremely difficult situation, in one of those moments in which you are really tested. Whom do you "obey" if you believe in the Ten Commandments? "Thou shalt not kill" is the really tough one to break when you're ordered to do it; you will always have to live with and bear responsibility for your decision, for your actions, and for the consequences. So I hesitated. I disobeyed the pilot's order and didn't open fire. In response, the pilot swung the chopper around 180 degrees so that the other gunner could open up on them. But, just at that moment, they dove from the sampan into the water, and I can only hope that they survived.

I will never know whether that old man and woman were Vietcong sympathizers or just South Vietnamese civilians who just happened to be in the wrong place at the wrong time. But there were other instances when I witnessed the killing of what I knew to be innocent civilians; and, in these instances as well, I simply could not bring myself to participate in increasing the body counts. This was the turning point in my life, the point when I really began to wrestle with my conscience about the war — and I have been against the Vietnam War, against any war, from that time right up to this day.

As a result of the unlawful behavior of my fellow soldiers, I started observing a trend that suggested to me that the local South Vietnamese were retaliating in revenge against all of the U.S.-caused civilian deaths. As an example, one night I was standing outside taking a leak and gazing up at the stars, when suddenly, I heard a swishing sound over my head. Looking up in the direction of the sound, I caught sight of a rocket-type bomb, about 8 feet long, passing overhead. Following the bomb with my eyes, I watched as it made a direct hit on our Flight Control Operations Center, about 100 feet from where I stood. This was the facility in which all crewmembers were briefed on the missions ahead, and where they sat in red light to allow their eyes to adjust from normal daylight vision to night vision. The explosion sent dust and dirt flying my way, and I raced for the shelter of the bunker, with everyone else, where we remained until things quieted down.

On another occasion, on the very next day as it so happened, we were flying on a search mission. In the lead was a small OH-6A Cayuse helicopter, a "Loach," manned by a pilot and a gunner. The Loach was flying low, just below our chopper at about 2 o'clock, when it suddenly blew up in mid-air. Later, it was discovered that hand grenades, wrapped in tape to hold the safety lever, had been dropped into the Loach's fuel cells. The JP4 aviation fuel, highly flammable and highly corrosive, in the cells dissolved the tape, setting off the grenades, the resulting explosion and fire incinerating both the pilot and the gunner. What's ironic is that these two particular individuals also happened to be at the top of the list for numbers killed. Coincidence?

Only a South Vietnamese civilian worker within the compound could have performed this act of sabotage undetected during the daytime, when it likely occurred. Likewise, the rocket attack could only have been planned and staged by civilians on base, who could have unobtrusively paced off, on foot, the range and trajectory necessary to score a direct hit on the Flight Control Operations Center.

In any event, you can imagine how nerve-wracking all this was to me when you consider that, during our flights; I sat right next to the chopper's fuel cells. Moreover, all of this was happening during the final month of my tour of duty in Vietnam, a busy time in which I was involved in everything from the insertion and extraction of troops, to picking up the wounded. So close to the end of my tour, I was more anxious than ever to get the hell out of there, and more afraid than ever that I wouldn't make it.

As a result of my refusal to kill, my commander assigned me to a duty reserved only for insubordinates: The Shit Detail. In this, you burned the human waste collected in the makeshift toilets used by the soldiers — steel drums, cut in half, with boards serving as toilet seats. Or, as we called them, the "Shitters." You poured diesel fuel into the drums, set the fuel on fire, and stirred the burning shit-diesel mixture until it was totally consumed. This was a stinking punishment usually reserved for those who, broken by the trauma of war, were too stressed out to go on combat missions.

Competition is a part of our society. We compete at everything we do to get ahead in life. We are taught to kill our competitors. It is a human fascination, this killer instinct of ours, that makes humans such good killers. It is no wonder that we are so obsessed with war, and think nothing of killing anyone who gets in the way of our accomplishing our agendas, our big goals in life. Dwight D. Eisenhower said the following about War:

> Every gun that is made, every warship that is launched, every rocket that is fired, signifies — in the final sense — a theft from those who hunger and are not fed, those who are cold and not clothed. This world in arms is not spending money alone. It is spending the sweat of its laborers, the genius of its scientists, and the hope of its children. This is not a way of life at all, in any true sense. Under the cloud of threatening war, it is humanity hanging on a cross of iron. I hate war as only a soldier who has lived it can, as only one who has seen its brutality, its futility, its STUPIDITY.

One day, while on the Shit Detail and on my way to the Shitters, I passed by a soldier, clad in nothing but his underwear, who was sitting in a chair in a pool of Agent Orange. I asked him why he was there. He said it was because he refused to go on any

19

more combat missions, and that this was his punishment for being insubordinate. It seemed to me so insane to do this to a human being simply for his not wanting to kill anyone. Why are humans so cruel to each other?

CHAPTER FIVE
HOUSE OF ABANDONED ANGELS

Seeing this soldier sitting in the chair took me back to when I was a little boy of four, living in an orphanage in Claremont, Virginia — a time, a memory, that will stay with me forever. There were a lot of us abandoned children at this orphanage. We all slept in the same room in separate fold-up cots. The orphanage was run by a couple, a man and a woman, in their home.

On that fateful night I will always remember, after we had been put to bed, I was still talking to the child next to me after the lights were out. Suddenly the man came up and yanked me out of bed, whipping me as he dragged me, screaming, to the door and out to the porch. The night was pitch black, and all I could see were the fireflies, the lightning bugs. Sitting me in a chair in the middle of the porch, he ordered me not to move or else he would whip me some more.

He then proceeded to walk around the house, pretending he was a monster coming to get me. He slowly crept along outside of the porch, making growling sounds and scraping the side of the house. Then he slowly opened the screen door and began walking towards me, looking like a towering dark shadow, his arms extended. Freaking out, I dashed back to my bed and dove under the covers. For a long time after that I was terrified of the dark. It was only much later in my life when, living in a teepee in Maine; I walked into the woods on my first night there, and finally came to realize how deeply this experience had impacted me. But that's another story.

When I think of that night, I think of UFOs, Unidentified Flying Objects. I imagine fireflies, lightning bugs, those glowing orbs of light that would come out in the summer. To me they were the lights of fairies, of supernatural beings, that would come and comfort me. And on that night of terror, I called on them.

All of this cruelty that humans harbor is a strange psychopathological dysfunction that seems to arise from deep-seated insecurities and fears manifested in the strangest behavior. For example, the reason I was in the orphanage in the first place was because Dad had left me with my grandparents, who made it obvious that they didn't want me around, then he up and disappeared for an extended period of time.

I think my issues with authority stem from being abandoned as a child. When you are abandoned you never have anyone telling you what to do. My response toward authoritarian people, toward those who like to tell others what to do, is this: Don't tell me what do unless I give you permission to tell me what to do.

CHAPTER SIX
THE RACCOON

My grandparents were Maude Lulu Harrison and Fletcher Evert Harrison, whom I called Grandmom and Granddad. After Dad left me with them, it soon became obvious to me that they felt burdened by me, and they often argued about who would watch me. This is a memory that has always bewildered me, especially when I think about how Granddad dealt with me so cruelly. For example, one day Granddad was about to go out the door when Grandmom insisted that he take me with him. He wasn't happy about me tagging along because, it turned out, he was going to see one of his girlfriends.

Later, as he romped around in bed with his girlfriend, I wandered around the house, listening to them moaning and groaning. Presently, I found my way into the bedroom where they were. I stared at them for a moment until Granddad told me to find something to do with myself. Walking into the clothes closet, I started trying on shoes. Finding a pair of cowboy boots, I put them on and walked around until he had finished his business. Then we left.

Upon our return home, Grandmom noticed the boots and wanted to know where I had gotten them and who had given them to me. I told her I had gotten them from the house of the lady with whom Granddad had been in bed. Now, mind you, I was only four years old. What did I know about cheating on one's wife?

A heated argument ensued between Granddad and Grandmom that seemed to go on forever. Suddenly Granddad grabbed me by the arm and stomped out the door. Outside, he threw me into the front seat of his pickup truck. Down the road we drove, in silence, until we arrived at the black water swamps where he kept his flat-bottomed boat, which he used for fishing and for trapping otters, minks, and raccoons.

He ordered me onto the boat, and I moved to the front as he shoved off with a paddle. It was a beautiful day, the sunlight shimmering on the water, the sun sparkling through the cypress trees. Moss hung from the cypress branches, and cypress knees extended above the water. I was immersed in the magic of the moment as we glided through the trees. Suddenly we came upon a raccoon sitting on a fallen tree in the water ahead of us.

Seeing us, the raccoon began to cry out for help, and I noticed that its foot was caught in a trap. The captive animal was looking at me imploringly, as though it hoped I could help it. I felt so sad. Abruptly Granddad turned the boat, swung himself up next to the raccoon, and proceeded to beat it to death. The animal's screams were painful to hear. This was a horrifying and upsetting act to witness, and it left me in shock. Then he turned towards me. Shaking the paddle at me, blood dripping from it, he said, "If you ever tell on me again, this is what I will do to you. You understand me?" With that, he turned his head to the side and spit tobacco juice into the water.

From that moment on, I never trusted Granddad again. He was a monster, and ours was a confusing relationship. Although I loved my Granddad, I was afraid of him. After this I was placed into the orphanage. And there I stayed until Dad came and rescued me from that house of abandoned angels.

CHAPTER SEVEN
MOONSHINE, BLOOD, AND SPAGHETTI SAUCE

I was now with Dad again and he was my hero, having rescued me from my orphanage nightmare. As mean as the man and woman were who ran the orphanage, because I was a child the trauma passed quickly from my consciousness. Riding in Dad's 1949 Ford, standing on the front seat and leaning on the dashboard, I was on the road again. On the car radio Hank Snow was singing, "Big train coming down the road, I'm telling you baby I'm moving on," as Dad sang along.

Dad's first stop was a regular one he often made, at a house where a robust black woman was sitting on the front porch in a swing. I remember that I was really glad to see her. She said, "Come here to me boy, I know what you need." I ran into her arms, she snuggled me up in her bosom, and pulled out one of her big, soft, warm breasts. Suckling on it, I fell fast asleep in her arms. In retrospect, I sense that Dad was having an affair with her.

That evening, Dad and I were driving down a long dirt road in the Suffolk County area of Virginia. The road seemed to go on forever, winding and turning. It was dark, and all you could see was what was illuminated in the headlights, and the brush alongside the road. This was backcountry, and you really had to know where you were going because there were no road signs marking the way. At times the road even disappeared. Finally, we came to an open area where a fire was visible. Dad stopped the car; we got out, and walked up to a couple of old black men who were sitting around the fire. The men called Dad by his nickname, Windy. We joined them at the fire, and they passed Dad a clear jar bottle of White Lighting — moonshine, corn liquor.

It all makes sense to me now, but at the time I had no idea what was going on; it was just a wild adventure and all that mattered to me was that I was with Dad again. He could just as well have been Robert Mitchum in the movie *Thunder Road*, a moonshine runner enjoying a jolly gathering around the fire with a couple of old bootleggers. We were back on the road making his deliveries, and it was exciting.

Later that night I was fast asleep in the front seat, when I was awakened by the car rocking, accompanied by moans and groans coming from the back seat. Peering over into the back seat, all I could see was a naked butt and testicles bouncing around. Dad had stopped at one of his honky tonk spots for some square dancing, and had gotten lucky and was romping with some woman in the back seat. Presently, Dad and the woman got out of the car and he put me in the back seat, giving me a shot of whiskey to put me to sleep. I didn't remember this part, but later he told me that I had thrown a Coke bottle at one of the car windows, breaking the window, because I was pissed off that he had left me in the car.

I found my way into the dance hall and remember hearing the "Tennessee Waltz" playing. About this time a big ruckus erupted and a fight broke out. It turned out that Dad had messed around with another man's woman, and now the brawl was on. Dad and the man were both fighting mad. Dad ended up being struck in the mouth with a baseball bat that knocked out one of his front teeth. Bleeding pretty badly, he grabbed me up and we made a hurried exit out the front door. Jumping into the car, we took off down the road, our tires squealing.

Our next stop was the house of Dad's Uncle Dick and Dick's wife, Dot. If you were to cast someone to play Uncle Dick, it would be Harry Dean Stanton. Dad needed to clean up and mend his wounds, so we spent the night. The next morning Uncle Dick went off to work, and Dad decided to go shopping for food in order to make dinner for everybody that evening. After Dad returned, he started preparing a spaghetti meal. As the afternoon progressed, and after a couple of glasses of moonshine were imbibed, Dad and Dot ended up humping on the couch. Dad and his aunt, my great-aunt, doing it. Having earlier fallen asleep in a chair, I was awakened by the noise of the throes of their passion, just in time to catch the last moment before orgasm.

Finished, they straightened themselves up, returned to the kitchen, and continued cooking dinner. By the time the table was all set and the food was done, they were all giggly. Uncle Dick returned home from work to find Dad and Dot pretty drunk. Uncle Dick was immediately suspicious, suspecting what had transpired, and he started arguing with Dot, smacking her around and threatening Dad. Soon a fight broke out between Dad and Uncle Dick, things started flying, and the table ended up being knocked upside down. Now all of our dinner was on the floor.

Grabbing a knife, Uncle Dick tried to stab Dad. Struggling, they bounced off the walls, knocking things off the counter, then fell on the floor in a heap and rolled around. Dot screamed as Dad and Uncle Dick wrestled for the knife. Soon, both Dad and Uncle Dick were covered with spaghetti sauce, looking like bloody messes. Finally Dad managed to knock Uncle Dick silly long enough to grab me and get the hell out of there.

In later years, Uncle Dick took his own life, blowing his brains out with a shotgun. I can only imagine how very difficult it was for him to live with himself. He abused Dot frequently, and almost beat her to death. He was also an alcoholic; and, when on good terms, he and Dad would go to bars, get drunk together, and pick up women.

CHAPTER EIGHT
GREAT GRANDMOM'S FARM

Sitting in the car, I could see that Dad was badly shaken up, spaghetti sauce all over him. Gathering his composure, he tried to figure out what to do next. Presently, he decided that his best course of action would be to take me to live with my Great Grandmom, Novella Estella Harrison, on her country farm in Claremont, Virginia. His decision made, we drove to Great Grandmom's farm.

Great Grandmom was a tall, lean woman who had lived all of her life on the farm, which had provided everything she needed to survive. She had a cow, a mule for tilling the land, some chickens, and a well for water. She had no electricity, but a wood stove provided heat. She grew all of her own food in her garden. Outside, she had an icebox, replenished by deliveries from the iceman, an elderly black man who delivered the ice by horse and wagon. Great Grandmom's land had been in the family ever since her ancestors had settled in the New World to start a new life. "This land is your land, this land is my land . . . This land was made for you and me."

Great Grandmom's farmhouse was a three-room wood structure, sitting on stilts, with a tin roof. The kitchen was separated from the sleeping rooms. Around the house was a porch. The house was tucked away in the forest, near a great fishing stream filled with trout. I enjoyed swimming in the deeper pools of the stream. I also had great fun swinging out over the stream on a rubber tire that served as a makeshift swing, and diving off the tire into the refreshing, cool, clear water. Yee-Hah! A buck-naked, red-headed, freckle-faced boy playing freely in pure carefree joy amidst the splendor of nature. A scene that could have come straight out of a Norman Rockwell painting.

Completing this rustic setting were lots of flowers, and two oak trees. Less flowery, though, were the farm's toilet facilities. At night, we used a bucket by the bed. Some distance from the farmhouse stood an outhouse, so old and decrepit that it leaned to one side. Inside the outhouse was a board, with a hole in it, which functioned as a toilet seat. The hole was bigger around than my little butt, and I remember that whenever I sat on the board I was always afraid I would fall into the stinky waste, which had accumulated in the outhouse pit for at least 100 years.

Toilet paper was a luxury we didn't have, and so as a substitute we used pages from old Sears and Roebuck catalogs. When no catalogs were available, we used dried-up corn shucks.

Another fun feature of the outhouse was that, in the spring, we had to watch out for hornet's nests.

People who have some ancestral connection to the Mayflower make such a fuss about the Puritans. My only claim to historical fame is that I share my last name with the likes of William Henry Harrison (1773–1841), the 9th President of the United States, and his grandson, Benjamin Harrison (1833–1901), the 23rd President of the United States.

On the other hand, based on the broader meaning of ancestry held by Native Americans, I am also related to Abraham, to Chief Joseph, to Martin Luther King, Jr., and to Nelson Mandela. And, combining the Native American concept of ancestry with the words of the Doobie Brothers, guess who my brother is? "Jesus is just all right with me, Jesus is just all right, oh yeah . . ."

However, I would be just as happy knowing that I was the descendant of some anonymous stowaway aboard some pirate ship, running from some dogma-barking oppressive religion. Look where organized religion, the relationship between State and Church, has gotten us. After thousands of years of violence and war, we are still fighting in the name of

GOD. My GOD will kick your GOD'S ass! Oh, yeah? Well MY GOD will nuke YOUR GOD'S ass into oblivion, so there!

In my travels, I invariably encounter someone who asks me how my ancestors obtained their land in Virginia. They HAD to have stolen it from the Indians, people tell me. I answer that my ancestors came over as homeless illegal immigrants, found a camping spot, and camped out. But don't you worry, I just say that my Great Grandmom sold her piece of land for an electric refrigerator, which caused me to become homeless, and so I am back to camping out like my ancestors.

My Grandmom was one of 12 children. One of her brothers, Cliff, had Down's syndrome and had lived on the farm with Great Grandmom since his birth. He did all the physical work around the farm. So here we were again, with Dad needing to find someplace to ditch me; and he talked Great Grandmom into leaving me with her on the farm for a while, until he could come up with some plan as to what the hell he was going to do next. Of course, I was sure she didn't like the idea. After all, she was 90 years old, had raised 12 children, and now, at this time in her life, had a 50-year-old child with Down's syndrome to look after, as well as the prospect of me, a four-year-old, to care for. A bit much at 90, but she agreed to let me stay. Or maybe she had no choice.

I fondly remember her cornbread, which she would make into cake patties that she cooked on the old black cast iron stove. She would put fresh-ground homemade peanut butter on the patties, which became my favorite food there.

Each day, she and I would get up before dawn. There was no heat in her house that early in the morning, and no insulation except for newspaper covering the walls. You could actually see light coming in through cracks in the walls. In the winter, the water basin would freeze over at night, and in the morning she would use an ice pick to break the frozen ice in order to reach the freezing cold water, which she used to wash her face. Looking back on it now, it was a hard life. But, being a kid, I didn't know any better, so I just took and accepted things as they were. At the same time, though, it was a healthy life, and Great Grandmom outlived all the men in her life. She was married only once, and her husband had died young of a heart attack. What I heard was that lots of men had come calling on her, but she never got married again.

Up before light, she would milk the cow first thing, and her cats would gather around for a squirt of milk in their mouths. She would send me into the chicken coup to fetch the eggs, and I would hold my breath because the ammonia from the chicken crap smelled so strong. No, it wasn't an easy life; and if you wanted to eat you had to either grow or kill your food yourself, then prepare it to eat. But, as I said, it was a healthy life.

Cliff would gather the wood to make a fire so that Great Grandmom could heat the place and cook some grub. Communicating with Cliff was difficult. He would sit and talk to himself for hours, and the only way I could get his attention was with pantomime. And so were born my mime skills that would serve me well as a performer later in life. I could amuse him by imitating the farm animals, or by pretending to do something that he did such as cutting wood.

Living in the south in the country, we were always close to the woods and to dogs and cats as well. Consequently, before giving me a bath, Great Grandmom would always stand me, naked, on a stool and check me over thoroughly, from head to toe, for ticks.

I always like to joke about what I do. When asked, I answer that I work for the C.I.U., the Central Intelligence of the Universe. I say that I look for intelligent life on Earth. When asked what I've found, I say that I've discovered that ticks are smart; they hang out on the trails, on brush and branches, waiting

32

for warm-blooded species to walk by, then jump aboard for a feast of blood and free travel.

One day, Dad showed up with a woman named Rose, who would later become my stepmother. Dad had met her while working in Baltimore. Our first encounter was not what I would say was the start of a bonding kind of loving friendship. Rose was a sassy 17-year-old, still in high school. She was young, immature, and jealously possessive of Dad, and she didn't want to have around a child born to another woman. As a result, unfortunately, we didn't hit it off, to say the least, and we never got along afterwards.

The first thing she said to me was, "So you're the little red-headed devil I hear so much about. Well let me tell you right now, you little snot-nosed brat, if you don't do what I tell you I will beat the devil out of you." That set the tone for our relationship from that point on; we would never be compatible. She was the most violent person I've ever had the misfortune to know and to live with. It would be a few years after this first meeting before I would see her again.

Time marched on, moving into the future. One beautiful summer day, Great Grandmom sat me in the yard under some honeysuckles, and a butterfly landed on my finger. I remember this well because, while studying this magnificent creation closely, I saw my reflection in its eyes, a sight forever locked in my cellular memory. They say you can't remember anything before age three. However, I don't believe that, because images of things from the past, when I was very young, appear in my mind, at times triggered by some particular smell, sound, or scent associated with the memory. Another image was of the chickens feeding on insects and bugs around me, when suddenly a snake was crawling towards me. The chickens made such a fuss, like little mother hens, that they drove the snake away.

The cow would graze by the apple tree, and behind this scene you could see Great Grandmom in the garden picking fresh vegetables. I would waddle towards her, passing right underneath and between the cow's legs. Then I would follow her through the rows of plants. As she picked them, she would feed me some of them, and by the time we had walked through the garden I had eaten a good meal. She would pick fresh apples from the tree, and would make the best apple pie in the world. Cliff would get the ice cream maker out, and we would make homemade ice cream to go with hot pieces of the freshly baked apple pie.

Great Grandmom tilled the fields herself, walking behind the plow as it was being pulled by the mule, having total control over this tool that turned the soil. Although she was a frail woman, I wonder how many people today could operate a mule-driven plow. Down the road was a water mill, where she would get her corn ground for personal use, and trade any left over at the general store for salt, sugar, and flour, and for the cloth she used to make her own clothes. She always wore the same style of dress, a flower-patterned print with a lace collar, and she wore what I called black granny shoes.

One day Grandmom showed up at the farm. Great Grandmom walked out of the kitchen and stood on the porch, wiping her hands, which were covered with flour, on her apron. She had been rolling flour for dumplings. Passing the back of one of her hands across her forehead, she brushed a strand of hair out of her face, leaving some flour on her brow. Addressing Grandmom, Great Grandmom said, "You got to take this boy with you, he's too much for me to handle."

Great Grandmom Novella Estella Harrison, the author,
and Grandmom Maude Lulu Harrison.

CHAPTER NINE
THE CIRCUS

That was the final image I would ever see of Great Grandmom alive. Grandmom had come to pick me up in order to go see a movie in the town of Waverly, Virginia, where she lived. The movie was *The Circus*, starring Charlie Chaplin. This film had an enormous impact on me, one that would spark my passion for film and make me take up filmmaking later in my life. The silver screen would capture my imagination and the wonder of how it worked — light streaming out of a hole in the wall and projecting images onto a screen. This was the first time that I had ever seen anything like this in my life. Back in those days, no one had TV sets as yet; and so, you can imagine the deep and lasting impression that my first experience with moving pictures had on me.

Charlie Chaplin took me visually, for the first time, into a fascinating world full of mystery and curiosity. Moving images of an animated character bigger than life. I stood on my seat, leaning on the back of the seat in front of me, mesmerized as I reached out with my hand, trying to touch the magic light streaming above my head.

I never returned to Great Grandmom's farm. Instead, Grandmom and Granddad reluctantly took me in, and there I was stuck living in their house in Waverly.

A few years later, Great Grandmom passed away in her sleep at age 92. And, what was to follow in the wake of her death would become the most horrifying nightmare of my life. Her funeral was held on a rainy day, with everyone dressed in black and standing around holding black umbrellas. What I remember most vividly is the hole in which she was to be buried. It was gray, and full of rainwater. And, because her coffin was made of wood, her pallbearers had to stand on it in order to get it to sink. This was so traumatic for me to watch that, to this day, I do not like going to funerals. The idea of being buried in the ground is not very appealing to me. I would have preferred my final image of Great Grandmom to be that of her standing on the porch in the sunlight, in her flowered dress, brushing the lock of hair out of her face.

The day after seeing *The Circus*, I was playing in the backyard of my Aunt Julia's house, across the street from Grandmom's house. Grandmom was having a discussion about the fact that Dad had left me with Great Grandmom, which Grandmom was not happy about. While I was playing in the sandbox with a toy truck, I cut my right knee on a rusty nail. It broke the skin, and a small drop of blood came out of the puncture wound.

Crying, I ran immediately to the front of the house, where the elders were sitting and talking, and tried to crawl into Grandmom's lap. She pushed me away, saying, "Stop your crying. It's just a little scratch." It was more than just a scratch, however — much more. Quickly it grew increasingly painful, which made me cry harder. Distracted from her conversation by my crying, Grandmom grabbed me by the arm and headed across the street to her house, saying that if Dad were taking care of me like he should this wouldn't be happening.

Shoving me into the bedroom, she said, "You stay there until you stop crying. Now I don't want to hear any more out of you." With that, she locked the door and left. As I lay there in bed, my knee began to become inflamed and infected; and soon I was in agony, screaming from the pain. When Granddad arrived home, she told him what had happened to me. He checked on me; but now had come his opportunity for revenge on me for having reported to Grandmom his indiscretion with his girlfriend. Saying that I had gotten what I deserved, he left me alone in the room. But that wasn't all. Now Granddad and Grandmom had a perfect excuse, a way, to get Dad to come back and take me off their hands. So they called him in Baltimore, which was 350 miles away, and then ignored me until he drove up.

Entering the bedroom, Dad looked at my knee. He could readily see the shape my leg was in, that the infection had spread, and that I was on fire with fever. Granddad and Grandmom had made not the slightest effort to take me to a doctor; they were yet more examples of the dysfunctional personalities populating my life. They were the most stubborn, most hardheaded, people imaginable; and I was, sadly, the target of the animosity between them and Dad. Still, I have always been a loving and forgiving person. Thus, despite my grandparents' total lack of concern, affection, and compassion for me, even when I was so sick, I still loved them.

When a doctor finally saw me, he informed Dad that I was suffering from a serious infection, and immediately had me admitted to a hospital in Richmond, Virginia. Once I was there, the doctors told Dad that my leg would have to be amputated, otherwise the infection would spread and I would die. And this entire nightmare could have been prevented had my Grandmom just cared enough about me to clean my wound with soap and water in the first place. Dad refused to let them amputate my leg, however, and for the next six months I went through hell fighting gangrene. Six years old and here I was, left all alone in a hospital with complete strangers.

In order to keep me from getting up and moving around, so that my leg could heal, I had to be tied down in bed. Every day, they placed me on a cold metal table, illuminated by blindingly bright overhead lights, then inserted a big needle into my leg and withdrew puss. This procedure was so painful that they had to have four people hold me down because I would kick and scream and try to escape.

As a result of all this, to this day I still have problems with sensations emanating out of my right leg and running through my body. In addition, following my injury, strenuous physical activity, especially competitive sports, proved difficult. Nevertheless, in 1967, the military took me anyway, which goes to show how desperate they were for warm bodies to fight in the Vietnam War.

Eventually, I healed to the point where I could leave the hospital, and pleaded with Dad, "Please, Daddy, no more hospitals." Once I was discharged, Dad arranged to have me placed in a foster home in Richmond, Virginia, with a family that, to this day, I wish Dad had left me with. My foster parents were patient, good, kind, loving people who took me in with their two sons, and loved me like one of their own.

CHAPTER TEN
DAZE OF WHINES AND ROSE

Meanwhile, Dad had finally remarried, found a steady job, settled down, and moved into a home in Baltimore. One night he came to Richmond to retrieve me and take me back to Baltimore, where I would live with him, a violent, obsessive, alcoholic father, and with Rose, my new stepmother — the most abusive human being I have ever known in my life. Let me state here that I am sorry if, in these pages, I offend any of Rose's relatives and friends out there who may have loved her dearly. Although you may have had good relationships with her, my relationship with her was vastly different, was horrific. Like they say, you don't know a person until you live with them. Thus, although she might have chilled out in her later years, she was a veritable tyrant when younger.

This relationship was very uncomfortable for me because Rose had no patience with me. She was simply too young to deal with a seven-year-old boy who needed a lot of attention. I was a distraction from her obsession with her vanity, her personal ambitions, and her goals in life. And so I soon became the constant target of her frustration and anger. Whenever things didn't go her way, look out, because all of her frustration turned into hostilities directed at me. There was no discussion or debating with her; there was never an option. When we would be sitting at the dinner table together — which wasn't very often — if I was not sitting up straight, or if I was eating with the wrong utensil, or if I was talking with food in my mouth, she would smack me in the face with the back of her hand. Whap!

Dad was soon back to his wild playboy ways, staying out all night and spending all of his money on booze. This further fueled Rose's insane rage. She would get so angry over Dad's gallivanting about that she would take out her frustrations on me over the smallest, most trifling thing that displeased her.

41

Grabbing me by the arm and holding me, she would scream, "You fucking little bastard, I'll kill you!" while beating me into a daze, into unconsciousness — striking me on my back, my head, my face. She would become so enraged that she would completely lose her mind. Only after wearing herself out beating me would she come to her senses. Sometimes her sister, my Aunt Louise, who lived next door, would call her name, and this would snap her out of her rage. Often I had to take refuge with Aunt Louise and stay at her house; but then Rose would accuse her of having sex with me.

When Dad would come home and see what Rose had done to me, they would get into an argument, and then he would beat her up. It was a vicious cycle that went around and around like a merry-go-round — and when will it stop, nobody knows. One night Dad came home while Rose was standing on a ladder, washing the front window. As soon as he set foot in the house, she started yelling at him about being drunk and smelling like sex. "Why don't you stay home and help around the house sometimes?" she shouted, at which point Dad yanked her off the ladder and she fell to the floor. Then, grabbing the water-filled bucket that she had been using in her cleaning, Dad threw it through the window. "There!" he shouted. "The fucking window is clean!"

At this point she called the police, and soon police officers came knocking on the door. Dad answered the door and the officers came in. Dad became cool very quickly; he could be a very sensible fellow when he needed to be. He convinced the officers that there was nothing to worry about, that everything was going to be all right, that it was just a little family squabble. After the officers left, Rose went upstairs to the bathroom. I was sitting on the floor, watching TV, probably the Roadrunner with Wiley Coyote, my favorite cartoon; I could identify with Wiley Coyote always getting his ass kicked. Dad went downstairs, but soon returned with an axe in his hands.

42

I heard him walking down the hallway to the bathroom; and soon I heard Rose scream, "Are you out of your mind?" as he commenced threatening her with the axe and chopping a hole in the wall. With every chop he warned her, "Don't you ever call the fucking cops again on me, woman, or I'll kill you!" After all this he packed his clothes, got into the car, with me in tow, and we left Baltimore for Virginia. This scenario would repeat itself, back and forth, back and forth, for years.

On each of these occasions, Rose would come to Virginia, begging Dad to come back. Once, he picked her up at the bus station when I was in the back seat of the car. At that time, Dad and I lived in a trailer on his sister's property on Prosperity Road. As we were passing Camp Pendleton, an old military base, Dad and Rose were arguing. The next thing I knew, he reached over, opened the car door on Rose's side, and kicked her out of the car onto the side of the road. Then he drove off, leaving her behind. Dad could certainly instill fear. You see shit like this, and you're afraid of this person capable of such an act. Dad's father indulged in the same sort of intimidation as well, with such acts of violence as his beating to death of the raccoon. Doing stuff like that today would land you in jail.

I realized that Dad was a madman who used brute force to intimidate people, keeping them in fear. Only seven years old, what could I do? It was like a trap, and I was a prisoner. Like the wedding oath, "Till death do us part." I couldn't get away from him; and he always convinced people that he would behave. If I made a movie about all this, it would be a horror film. And I've already described my feelings about horror films.

Rose finally showed up at the trailer after having walked back. Apologizing to her, Dad asked her to forgive him. He did this crying thing, which he would always do in these situations; then they hugged and kissed, had sex, and everything was back to normal. He packed his things and then we all returned to Baltimore. For a while, things were good — and then his drinking started again.

43

We lived on Fourth Street, between Cambria and Pontiac Street, in Brooklyn Outer South, Baltimore, near the county line. Each night I would wait for Dad and Rose to go out for the evening. One night I was sitting on the toilet seat, leaning on the windowsill, listening to the back-alley action of the Bohemian folk in my neighborhood. Presently, I decided to sneak outside. "I be sneaking out the back door hanging out with hoodlums in the street," as Stevie Wonder would say.

Leaving the house, Dad and Rose went their separate ways, leaving me unsupervised, as they did all the time. I never had a baby sitter, and was always left alone. Never once did anyone put me to bed or read me a bedtime story. As soon as the front door closed, I ran to the front bedroom window and peeked out through the Venetian blinds, watching until they disappeared. Sometimes, Dad could disappear for weeks at a time, and it was not safe for me to be in the house with Rose when he was not around.

As soon as they were gone I flew down the stairs, a single leap propelling me to the bottom of the stairs. Bouncing off the wall, I flew through the air and out the back door. Running as fast as I could, I hurdled the gate at the end of the yard in a single bound. Landing on my feet, I made a quick left turn, still traveling at the speed of light. Now on the street corner, I surveyed everything that was happening. Making my choice as to what to do next, I stepped into a game of "Kick the Can," and I was "It." As I grew older, on nights like this I would sometimes bring my buddies home and we would head to the basement and get drunk on the homemade wine that Dad made in big hickory-smoked barrels.

Rose took my house key away from me so that I would have to wait until she got home from work before I could get into the house; so I would just roam the streets. When I came home I had to knock on the back door to get in. Sometimes, I would just forget about the time, and before I realized it, it was

44

dark. One time I rode my bicycle to the airport, which was located about 20 miles away from our house. To this day, I don't know how I found my way there, or how I found my way back home again.

Sometimes Rose would hide behind the back door, holding her torture instrument of choice, a metal fly swatter. She would use the wire end of it to strike my precious little body in a rage of violence. As a result, I eventually just wouldn't come home, and often ended up sleeping under the church steps. I would only return home when Dad was there, or he would come looking for me. He could always find me at the movies. In those days, a movie ticket cost 25 cents. To acquire the necessary quarters, I collected soda bottles and turn them in for refunds.

Often, when I had been beaten really badly, my schoolteacher would notice the puss stains on my shirt from the popped blisters on my back, and would usually send me to the school nurse's office. The nurse would ask me to take off my shirt so that she could use her stethoscope. Seeing the open wounds on my back, she would notify the social service people, who would then show up at the house. But Rose would threaten to kill me if I told them that she beat me. So, whenever they asked me if she beat me, I would always say no. Stupidly, they always interrogated me in front of her, so what else could I do?

On holidays Rose would always make me wear a suit and tie. On one such occasion, along with my suit, I had on new shoes, white bucks, and she insisted that I keep the outfit and the shoes on all day. Being a young kid, however, I wanted to play. The other kids decided that my new shoes needed to be scuffed up a little, so they stepped on them until they weren't clean anymore. When I returned home with my clothes dirty and my shoes scuffed up, Rose flew into one of her rages and beat the crap out of me. It was not unusual for me to suffer a beating daily.

I had a dog named Teddy Bear. One time Rose came home from work upset, and she flew into one of her rages. Taking me by the neck, she shoved my face into Teddy Bear's dog shit because I had not picked it up from the back yard. This angered me to the point that I wanted to kill her. To this day, whenever I see someone picking up dog poop, I feel rage over this inhumane disciplinary act inflicted upon me by Rose. Why would anyone do this to a child? I haven't had a dog since.

The author and Teddy Bear.

Another time, while I was coming home from school, a kid named Eddie Page picked up a rock and threw it at me, striking me in the head and busting a blood vessel. Soon, blood was squirting out of my head with every heartbeat. So there I was, walking around, trying to figure out what to do, as I couldn't get into the house without a key. Covered in blood, I went to the house of Rose's mother, who lived two doors down from us.

I knocked on her door, and she took me in and tended to my injury; but I just about bled to death, as she couldn't stop the bleeding. After a while, however, the bleeding stopped on its own. Around that time Rose, finding me there, came in screaming that she didn't want me in her mother's house. Grabbing my arm, she dragged me back to our house. It wasn't bad enough that I had just been struck in the head with a rock and had almost bled to death; now I was being punished for seeking help.

CHAPTER ELEVEN
HOLDING UP THE TOWEL

At this time in my life today, I realize that we really don't have much choice over our sexuality, any more than over the color of our skin. What is sex all about anyway? Is it a feeling? Look at procreation; you can have a baby without a partner. Diversity seems to be a part of the many species of the earthly erotic garden of the senses anyway. Expressing one's sexual interest without fear would seem to be a healthy act that promotes self-esteem. I could lie to you about the sexual curiosity I've had throughout my life, but telling the truth has always been the particular manifestation of my naiveté. I have fantasized about everything imaginable sexually, but I think that sex is highly overrated; it's always about business and money. You have to pay for sex, in one way or another, no matter how you look at it.

We are so addictive that we can become obsessed with anything. I was burned out on sex by time I was a teenager. I thought life was all about sex, drugs, and rock-and-roll. What's interesting is that I didn't actually have intercourse for the first time until I was 21. And it happened only because of peer pressure that I experienced while in the Army overseas. It's funny. Your peers bug the shit out of you, trying to get the inside dope about your sexual orientation. I'm not a good liar, and it wasn't until I went overseas, got laid, and lost my virginity that the guys stopped bugging me. Now I was one of the guys, a real man's man. Oh, man! When you are sexually active, you give off a vibe that attracts the opposite sex. It's something invisible that everyone can sense, especially women. It's like being a stud, hard like a rock all the time, ready to provide service, that attracts the ladies. To put it another way, the test has always been, when you're a man with a women, to hang a towel on your hard-on to see if it can hold up the towel.

Being bumped up all the time, always being on call to perform at the snap of the fingers, is too stressful for me. Life is short and I want to enjoy it. Time flies by so fast and then, one day, you wake up and look in the mirror, and your youth has faded away. We are only young, beautiful flowers for a short time. I want to relax and explore the magic of being here on Earth, of being in this physical world.

Love is strange concept. When I think of the relationship between my parents, I remember how Dad used to say to me, "You got to smack them around once in a while." There's a great scene in the movie *Mr. & Mrs. Smith* when Brad and Angelina are hunting each other down with bombs and guns. Finally, they come face to face in hand-to-hand combat. They beat the shit out of each other, and then fuck. There's also passion of the sort depicted in the movie *Passion*.

We humans are strange creatures; we suffer and then we feel guilty about it. That's what religion, to me, seems to be all about — making you feel guilty. There's a concept that a good relationship is a "mirror" that can only work when you have two intelligent, mature people having great respect for one another's dignity, not wanting anything but real love. Well, let's go and look into the mirror and love ourselves.

My current philosophy has evolved out of the life I have lived. When I look back, I realize how insecure my parents were just trying to figure life out. Life is complicated, and there is no manual to explain how it works or how to make it easier. After World War Two, every aspect of life took off and accelerated, and became more complicated. For example, look how technology has advanced by leaps and bounds over the last 50 years. It's really hard to keep up with technology today, and if you have no means to do so it can be frustrating. This is a material world with lots of things; we must have our "toys." As a result of the fast pace of everything, of trying to "keep up," love or sex can become rushed and frustrating, thereby turning into a big disappointment. This disappointment can eventually make you anxiety-ridden, which seems to be associated with the repression of anger. The result is sexual frustration, which often becomes a neurosis, fostering a guilty conscience that the marketing industry has plugged into. When we are depressed, we go out and spend money in the hope that buying things will somehow make us feel better about ourselves, will somehow fill the void left by sexual frustration.

Sex is the physical act by which we come into physical life, so it makes sense that happiness is all about our relationships with others. I really believe in the concept that "There is no sanctuary in one bed from the memory of another. The memories of faces preserved in the anger of hurt. Heart broken or heart breaker it brings back the haunting eyes of rejected lovers." We have to first love ourselves, first understand how to satisfy our own needs, before we can share with another person the experiences that loving intimacy offers. Sounds good, but humans are so unpredictable; we can shift gears in a second and change our minds.

There was no emotional intimacy between Rose and me. We never bonded, and there was no heart-felt love. Her insecurity poisoned her. She got caught up in jealousy, not understanding the relationship between a father and his son by birth and blood. In her mind, I was competing with her for Dad's attention. She also harbored a lot of anger over not fulfilling her goal of living the "American Dream." In addition, Rose never had any children of her own; there were a few "pro-choice" acts on her part, which, I believe, further fueled her resentment towards me. In a way she was like my real mother, who was never satisfied, and who abandoned several of her children until she found the man who would give her the lifestyle she wanted. Love is not fair.

There were both good times and bad times in our family. My parents could seem like the sweetest people in the world, but their behavior was unpredictable, not to be trusted, because they could change at any moment. One day, everything would seem okay; the next day, Dad and Rose would be raging out of control. After each of her outbursts of insane rage, Rose would always try to make up to me by being nice, by acting like nothing had happened. She would buy me some gift, but I stopped accepting these gifts because she would always take them away later, as punishment. It was a double-edged sword: If I took her gifts, she would take them back; if I didn't take them, it would piss her off and she would call me an ungrateful bastard.

Speaking of "gifts": Next door to us lived Rose's distant cousin, Virginia Gluck, and Virginia's husband, Harold, whom we called Aunt Virginia and Uncle Harold. They had a daughter named Beverly. When I reached my 13th birthday, Beverly was 16 and blossoming into a beauty. Her bedroom was right next to mine; and, having a real fascination with her, I had earlier taken a coat hanger and poked a hole in the wall so that I could peek through at her. Unfortunately, I never caught a clear view of "anything."

Anyway, although I hadn't had a birthday party in a while, there seemed to be some urgency in my family for me to be given a 13th birthday party. After arriving at the party, however, Uncle Harold took this opportunity to give me the "gift" of punishment: 13 spankings that really hurt. I suppose he did this because he discovered the hole in the wall. As a result of this, not only was that the last birthday party I ever had, I never spoke to Uncle Harold again. My family members could have talked to me about this, letting me know that they knew what I was doing, which would have made me feel bad enough and been sufficient punishment. After all, I was a young male coming into puberty, and a little understanding on their part could have helped me. But, of course, I was denied that understanding.

At 14 I ran away from home. In an effort to find me, Rose's niece Patsy, my older cousin, enlisted the aid of her Catholic priest, a close friend, to help in the search. On the night of the day in question, they finally tracked me down. A car chase ensued through the streets, ending in an alley. After talking with me, they convinced me to return home.

Once I was there, Rose launched into a dramatic performance, crying, "Why do you do this to me? It hurts me!" A convincing performance, but she quickly returned to her evil ways. I can't help but remember and compare this to Faye Dunaway's brilliant portrayal of Joan Crawford in the movie *Mommie Dearest*; check out the raging coat hanger massacre.

The interesting thing about this story is that Patsy ended up marrying the priest, and they had two children together. He was a really good man. Later, when I was about to be sent to Vietnam, he actually tried to get the necessary paperwork together for me to file as a Conscientious Objector. By the time the paperwork was in, unfortunately, I was already in Vietnam.

CHAPTER TWELVE
THE CHURCH THING

My parents did the church thing for a while. As a family we tried it, but my parents putting on a good face was both ironic and useless because my impulse to tell the truth would cause them embarrassment. My Sunday school teacher would ask me how things were at home, and I would tell the truth. Consequently, going to church didn't work out for my parents, and so their putting on good behavior didn't last very long. I stuck it out for a while, as it was fun being with God-worshipping people. I did the whole thing: Sunday school, Bible school, and summer Bible camp. That is, until the minister of the church was asked to leave because of inappropriate behavior; which is what caused me to lose my faith in religion at that early age. I even tried Scouting — the Cub Scouts, the Boy Scouts, the Explorers — until our den father became involved in an extramarital affair, which brought Scouting to an end for me.

My Grandmom was a southern Baptist, a fire-and-brimstone type. When she was around there was no swearing, no music. You could listen only to Billy Graham on the radio; and the only book in her house was the Bible. As an aside, I have always wondered why the only book in a hotel room is the Bible. Personally, Jesus seems to me to be all about being connected to the Inner Spirit. However, we have been disempowered by the church, and have thus ended up worshipping Jesus himself instead of the Inner Spirit. I do not understand religion and its theological authority, based on a shaky interpretation of history, claiming to be interested in the peoples' welfare. Yet religion is a pulpit subservient to the State, not to the welfare of individuals — a pulpit chained to illusions and swearing to God under a doctrine of mental reservation. Our welfare is actually gained through unregimented education, not through excommunication by ecclesiastical authority.

An interview of Ralph Steadman by Michael Simmon in the art magazine *ARTILLERY* included Steadman's comments on Hunter S. Thompson's empathy for the poor. Steadman noted that blind social religious obedience has created a schizophrenic society as a result of the emotional suppression of the human spirit. The ethical work state of mind has left many citizens impoverished, and people in poverty have no chance of financial success in life when state and church take the "rights of man" away.

Each individual should have the right of self-governance. We each treasure the freedom to live equally, to stand at the helm of our vessel, steady in every fiber of our star-being, a free spirit navigating our individual destiny through the minefields of bigotry and hatred arising from religious intolerance.

Picking up a piece to the jigsaw puzzle of my life and peering into a moment in time: I appeared in a scene in the TV pilot of *Windfall* in Los Angeles. During the scene, while seated at a banquet table on the set, I could see the reflection of my face in a polished metal dinner plate, which brought forth a reflection and a speculation. I asked myself: What times are these that should strain a poet's soul when reason with good sense is a sign of understanding? How do we see both sides of the story and not lose the capacity to love? There are so many different ways to interpret the human code. We have become lost in translation. Living has become so complicated that stress has become a way of life. The creation of slumbering conditions, in anticipation of alarming danger, fills the air with apprehension. Lost are harmonious relationships, replaced by a strange fearfulness in a wasteland of crushing grief and a gasping for the primal elements and life forces. When one loses touch with breath, that precious life-giving force, poeticism ceases to exist.

CHAPTER THIRTEEN
CLASS CLOWN

I had a very difficult time in elementary school. I had a short attention span; I was usually too tired to stay awake; and I was too depressed to learn anything. So the school administration placed me in a class composed of kids who had learning disabilities.

Moreover, the administrators weren't finished, arriving at the decision that I had a serious speech problem. What was really the case here, however, was that while I was at Great Grandmom's farm, I had picked up her and Cliff's dialect, which I would describe as "Rolling Hills of Appalachia Hillbilly Folk Language." The other kids found my speech entertaining, but the teachers placed me in speech therapy; and soon, I picked up "Proper English." You learn fast when you're a kid and people make fun of the way you talk.

School was like a war zone to me. Once, one of my teachers made a dunce out of me by sitting me on a stool, and making me wear a dunce cap, in front of the whole class. This gave my classmates the perfect excuse to insult and tease me, as well as to hurt me physically. As a result, I ended up losing interest in school and started skipping it. Later, I was expelled from elementary school because of my wild antics; on one of my report cards was written, "He thinks he is Red Skelton, always performing, doing anything to disrupt the class, making students laugh."

As far as my stepmother Rose was concerned, I wasn't going to amount to anything, and she would bang me on my head to remind me of that. I received no support at home; she would say, "You're going to end up in the streets, a fucking bum." So, to spite her, I started dressing up like the Red Skelton character, Freddy the Freeloader, going out on the streets, and acting like a bum. This was fun for a while. But after I got eggs

57

thrown at me, got spat upon, and got beaten up, the novelty wore off in a hurry.

Rose refused to help me with my school lessons. And I couldn't ask Dad to help me with my lessons because he hadn't made it past the third grade, and was seriously self-conscious about his lack of education. Plus, he was never around anyway. So I ended up not doing my homework at all.

There were gangs in my neighborhood when I was growing up, and if you were in the wrong place at the wrong time you could literally be killed. To survive the mean streets, I became the Class Clown and the Street Clown. It was a matter of, "Make me laugh, clown, or I'll beat you up." So I developed a reputation by standing on street corners, under streetlights, under the spotlight if you will, entertaining the gangs. The gang members would even look for me just for their personal amusement. It was tough being me, a skinny redhead, and I had to be really fast on my feet and fast with my wit. Later on, as an adult, I adopted the performance name of "Street Corner Mime."

Let me share with you an insight about The Spotlight. It's amazing to me how, one moment, The Spotlight is shining upon you: You're in The Spotlight. But then, the moment passes, and The Spotlight fades out, and you find yourself all alone, at a crossroads in life, in the dark. Lost in thought, you realize that you cannot violate the laws of physics and exist in Zero Time, cannot live perpetually within that lost moment in which you were bathed in The Spotlight's brilliant illumination. The conflict here is that matter — that you — are carried along by the relentless flow of time, and cannot exist as a singularity, forever frozen and dwelling within a given happy moment under The Spotlight.

Now I perform under a different spotlight, the Divine Light, which lights my inner fire, which sets my soul on fire, which ignites my ecstasy. I experienced these feelings during a relationship with a woman, but ended up finding myself holding my broken heart, a thousand pieces of feelings and confused emotions, in my hands. She asked me, "Why don't you love me like before?" But she could never understand the reason why.

My faith in trust, my confidence in character, and my belief in the strength of romantic love and the future it creates are broken. Gone are the dreams of hope formed in relationships entrusted to one another, giving rise to emotional license to believe that romantic love is real, not an illusion. But romantic love is, indeed, just an illusion, and is, like light, like The Spotlight, limited and transient. So now I embrace the Divine Light, the Light of Divine Intelligence, which spawns the wisdom of "I Am," the pure consciousness of spirit. Love — pure love, far above the imperfections of romantic love — is the greatest force in the Cosmos, in the ethereal planes of elemental atomic consciousness that keep us in motion. Life is a balancing act of patience and tolerance, of unselfish understanding, of self-realization. When one is single, one is light, one is enlightened, one is no longer empty.

A flaming light from a distant star awakens my peaceful heart. A restored love inspires my faith in the hope that anything is possible, and I trust that "I am" honoring the miracle of the Goddess Mother of "ALL" creation, who lives within all that is. I am now truly free to live that which is most important, the precious gift of life. No more abandonment issues. No one is responsible for my needs for I have found, in the service of "PEACE," all that I need.

My experiences during my childhood street corner miming shattered whatever illusions I might have had that my world was a safe one. Once a gang caught me in an alley while I was on my way to the movies, and they tied me up. After removing my clothes to see whether I was a boy or a girl, they threatened me with a knife, saying they were going to skin me alive. They tried to pull my red hair out to see if it was real, and

59

then they gave me a "Pink Belly," meaning that they spanked me on my stomach until it turned red. Following this incident, Dad cut my hair off, making it as short as the fuzz on a tennis ball.

Having red hair can be interesting. Because of my red hair, I have been given many nicknames: "Pinky Boy," because of my skin color; "Red-Headed Devil"; "Woodpecker"; "Carrot Top"; "Red Top"; "Freckle Face"; "Penis Head"; and, the weirdest of them all, "Red on the Head like a Dick on a Dog." People talk about minority groups, but you never hear anything about redheads; yet we are the smallest minority group in the world. There was even a period in history when red-haired babies were killed because such children were believed to be the sign of the Devil. What a bunch of bullshit. Humans are the most dangerous creatures on the planet, with a long historical track record of inflicting discrimination and genocide on other humans for the flimsiest of reasons, such as skin color. Or hair color.

In junior high I completely lost interest in school, and stopped going. By this time the bullies were getting tougher and meaner. When I would come home crying after getting beaten up, Dad would tell me that I had to learn to stand up for myself, to be tough, to go back out there and fight back. But fighting was not my specialty. I preferred doing something creative. Besides, had I fought back, I would have just ended up getting into more trouble.

I loved to act out things that I saw in the movies or on TV. I would create a costume or a prop, and then go out on the streets as a knight or a cowboy. But the bullies would always come and destroy my props. Being a superhero only worked on the big screen or on TV.

By the time I was a teenager, I was drinking like Dad, trying to gain his approval by being like him. Soon, however, my drinking was out of control because it was easier to join the crowd than to fight the temptations. My parents weren't good role models; they always said, "Don't do as we do, do as we tell you." Yeah, right.

My life was wasting away, and I was on the fast track to becoming a juvenile delinquent, spending most of my time on the streets getting into trouble. At the same time, however, I was forming family-bonds with other abused kids. Once, when I was 15 and running with the wrong crowd, I actually got picked up by the police for drunk and disorderly conduct. I was really lucky that I never ended up in jail.

Dad got me my first job, which was working in a restaurant, washing dishes. Dad knew the restaurant's owner, which is how I got the job. However, it didn't last long, and I then applied for a job at the Shipyard at Maryland Dry Dock. I got the job by lying about my age, putting down that I was 16, on the application. At the time I was still really skinny, so I could crawl through the hatches of boilers, carrying an air jackhammer. My job was to break up the firewalls inside the boilers, using the jackhammer, and then toss the burned-oil residue out the hatch. It was a dirty job that lasted through the summer.

In the winter months, I worked evenings at a grocery store, called Giles Market, on Patapsco Avenue. Working the register one night, the time came for my break. Another employee, George Hall, who was also a friend, relieved me. Later, upon returning from my break, I learned that in my absence the store had been held up; someone had entered with a gun and robbed the register. During the course of the robbery George, who was manning the register, was shot in the liver and was rushed to the hospital in critical condition. Fortunately, George recovered from his wound. For the rest of my life, however, any job I had that required my operating a cash register brought back this memory, causing me to have a panic attack whenever I found myself alone to close the register and count the money. I would freak out, so such jobs never lasted long for me.

The first big lesson in my life I learned at Charlie's Pool Hall, located around the corner from where we lived. One day, after getting my week's pay from Giles Market, I went to the pool hall. There, I got hustled by a pool shark, who took me for my entire paycheck, for $60.00. The lesson here was clear: Never try beating a man at his own game.

On one of the occasions when my parents left me home alone, some friends of mine came to the house. We started drinking, and finally I passed out on the couch — a situation that very nearly turned into a disaster. As it turned out, some of those guys weren't my friends after all. While I lay unconscious, they turned on the gas burners and left. The row houses in which we lived were referred to as "matchboxes" because they were wooden and dry, with wallpapered walls. Highly flammable. A natural gas explosion in my house would have caused a fire that could have burned down our entire block of row houses. Luckily, Dad happened to come home to pick up something he had forgotten. Realizing the gravity of the situation, he turned off the burners and opened up the windows and door to get air circulating through the house. A close call.

For a time I had a newspaper route. Delivering papers in the summer wasn't bad, but making deliveries during the winter was something else entirely. The winters in Baltimore brought severe, freezing, biting cold weather. One winter morning, while picking up my papers, I sat down on a stack of them, and set about folding and putting rubber bands around the papers. In the middle of this task, I drifted off to sleep. Fortunately, my paper boss just happened to drive by, checking to see if I had shown up, and he got to me and roused me in time to prevent me from freezing to death. I will never forget this experience. Incidentally, frostbite is very painful, especially if you put your hands under hot water, which makes the pain even worse.

In order to finish junior high, I went to night school; then I entered my first high school, Southern High. During my second semester in the tenth grade there, I managed to get myself thrown out of school for running around naked during swimming class. This happened on a day when the doors to the school's Olympic-sized pool were open. These doors opened up to the houses on the street, so whenever they were open, people outside could see everything that went on around the pool. Now it so happened that we had to swim naked in the pool for reasons unknown. And the school administrators should have known the potential problems that could arise from combining naked teenaged boys with doors that opened to the outside world.

On the day in question, I arrived at the pool area to see that the doors were open. Needing to get to the other side of the pool, I started running, stark naked, passing right by the open doors. Midway there, being the goofball that I am, I suddenly stopped and launched into a little jig, shaking and gyrating my whole body for everyone outside on the street to see. Observing this, the swimming teacher escorted me to the Principal's Office. As punishment I was expelled, booted out of the school, and ended up transferring to City High School. To this day, I find it strange that we had to swim naked in the pool; this would not be allowed in schools today.

During my senior year at City High, I was playing football with some buddies in the street, when I tried to tackle this guy who was twice my size. He struck me in the throat with his elbow and knocked me to the ground. Sustaining a crushed Adam's apple and a ruptured larynx, I ended up in the hospital for a few weeks, and was told that I would never talk again.

High school was always a challenge for me. My diet was poor, I had no support at home, and, most of the time, I had to hitch a ride to school because I had no bus fair. In 1967 I received my high school diploma "out the back door," meaning that they just cut me loose. I was out of school, only to be drafted into the armed forces by the end of that summer.

In Maryland I spent my summers at Ocean City, hanging around the beach, surfing, enjoying the freedom of summer. And now, in 1967, here I was in my last summer at Ocean City, my last summer to enjoy the freedom of my youth. Hanging out on the beach around campfires, we'd sing such folksongs as "If I Had a Hammer." ("If I had a hammer, I'd hammer out a warning, I'd hammer out danger, I'd hammer out love between my brothers and my sisters, all over this land. It's the hammer of justice; it's the bell of freedom.") The Beatles' *Sgt. Pepper's Lonely Hearts Club Band* was one of my favorite albums, one that I would listen to over and over again. On the day that my draft notice arrived, Dad came to the beach to deliver it to me; then he took me back to Baltimore, where I reported to the recruiting office. Rose seemed happy about my going into the military; she said it would straighten me out, make a man out me.

My mantra, from The Beach Boys, was "Good . . . Good . . . Good . . . Good Vibrations." But now the Good Vibrations were over. And, for the next few years, I would be marching to vibrations that were anything but good.

CHAPTER FOURTEEN
I'M IN THE ARMY NOW

Going into the Army took me away from the problems that had consumed my life up to that time. Military service was my way out of a poor neighborhood, a neighborhood in which the only jobs available were in the chemical factories. Once you're in the Army, it is really difficult to get thrown out; they just kick your ass when you fuck up and don't do what they tell you to do. For example, I was trying to be funny in the mess hall one morning, and the drill sergeant reamed me out. The military has no sense of humor. He saw me as someone with an attitude, not as a clown. He made the entire company stand at attention, waiting for me, while I low-crawled on my stomach the entire distance from the mess hall to my platoon, which was the last one in the company formation. The distance was a good 500 feet. When I finally reached my platoon, he barked, "Fifty push-ups right now, soldier!" After I knocked out the push-ups, he stood over me, yelling all kinds of obscenities at me; then he ordered me to get into formation and stand at attention.

Getting right in my face, he launched into a tirade, yelling that I was a disgrace to the Army because my fatigues were dirty, my boots were scuffed, and my belt buckle was scratched. But what did he expect, after forcing me to crawl 500 feet on my stomach on the ground? Continuing, he made me dig my grave under the barracks; if you saw Stanley Kubrick's film, *Full Metal Jacket*, my situation could have been a scene straight out of the movie. I would dig the perfect hole, about my height, then another drill sergeant would come along and ask me what the hell was I doing, digging a hole under his barracks? He would then order me to fill the hole back up. And so it went on like this, me digging and filling, digging and filling, all night long.

The Army did get me back on track for a while — until, that is, they sent me to Vietnam. At first, Nam wasn't so bad because they initially sent me to an in-country Rest and Recuperation (R&R) town named Vung Tau on the China Sea. The first thing I did after checking into my unit was to find the South China Sea. I had heard that the Australians had a base by the water there; that the surf was good sometimes; and that they had a club on the beach, complete with surfboards. Once I discovered this hidden little paradise, I started spending a lot of time there — too much time, actually, as far as my superiors were concerned.

Walking down the beach one day, I met a sweet, beautiful Vietnamese girl, who lived on the beach in a palm hut. We hit it off, and I started hanging out with her, spending my evenings on the beach watching spectacular sunrises. It was here that I lost my virginity, to her. It was a good life, but that would soon change. My superiors sent in the Military Police, the MPs, to retrieve me; and, after less than two weeks in Vung Tau, I was shipped out to the Mekong Delta, where I spent the rest of my tour in Nam.

I have suffered from depression all of my life. In Nam, however, I wasn't yet aware of this as I am now. Also, depression simply wasn't an option there. The first time I found myself in the middle of a firefight, with bullets whizzing by me, explosions going off all around me, and everything on fire, I didn't have the time to panic or to give in to fear and crippling emotions. Had I given in to fear, I wouldn't be here now. My depression took a back seat to my survival instincts.

On the subject of fear, one fear that has taken me a lifetime to deal with is stage fright. Episodes of stage fright would make me feel sick, like I was going to throw up. My heart would be pounding, and I would get the shakes so bad that my knees would go weak and wobbly on me, making it hard for me to walk. To learn how to control and deal with my stage fright, I took a workshop in Sacred Acting with Elisa Lodge at Esalen Institute in the mid-1980s. Elisa wrote the book on Expressive

Arts Fitness, entitled *Primal Energetic*, and she is an inspiring teacher. In her book she writes about her experience in Actors Studio in New York City, where she was in class with Marilyn Monroe. Elisa was shocked to see Monroe struggling with stage fright. However, Monroe concealed her fear by slowing down her vocal tempo and gestures, and in so doing she achieved that famous combination of fragility and heightened sexuality that made her so famous.

Back to the war, to take my mind off the fear I experienced as a soldier, I would look through magazines at pictures of places I wanted to see when I returned to the States. These pictures, and the dreams of travel they conjured up, helped sustain me until, finally, in 1969; my tour of Nam came to an end.

During my weeklong trip out of Vietnam, I was exhausted from lack of sleep, as the Vietcong were mortaring us every night. During a stop in Saigon on my way out, I visited the "50/50 Ward" in a military hospital. This ward housed those patients given a 50-percent chance of recovering from their injuries, including soldiers who had lost most, or all, of their limbs in combat. I wanted to see how a particular pilot I knew was doing, who had been injured a few weeks earlier when his Bell AH-IG Cobra Gunship Helicopter had lost its main rotor while we were flying a mission. As a result of the malfunction, the chopper had dived into the ground, and the pilot had been blown right out of the chopper on impact, which broke every bone in his body. Standing at his bedside, looking at his broken body covered from head to toe in a cast, I also took in the smells of open wounds, took in the sights of all these young men, many now amputees, just sitting there, distant gazes in their eyes. Heart wrenching and depressing beyond my ability to describe in mere words. Stepping outside, I vomited. This was the last straw, the one that broke me. I still have a hard time emotionally when I recall this period of my leaving Nam and returning to the States.

During the plane flight home, there was nothing but dead silence. No one said a word.

Finally arriving home, I saw that my parents had put up a "Welcome Home" banner on the house. Dad had actually worried about me a lot while I was in Vietnam; it had dawned on him that I could have gotten killed there.

As stressed out as I was upon my arrival, I do remember that when I arrived home there was a parade. My Sunday school teacher, Mrs. Farrell, by then a sweet elderly woman, had arranged for me to appear in a ceremonial event in uniform. I remember stepping up on stage and Mrs. Farrell embracing me in a warm hug. In Sunday school she had taught me the virtues of life; and now, looking into her kind eyes, emotions welled up inside me and tears started rolling down my cheeks. Looking out at all the faces of the people in my community, the full impact of my experiences in Vietnam, my inner conflict about the war, the realization that the war had stolen my innocence, spiraled throughout my body. As a result, standing there, I was speechless, unable to say anything, and I began to question my sanity. I was handed a wreath of flowers, which I placed on the local war memorial later that same day. Although grateful to be alive and safely home, while standing at the memorial I felt paralyzed, weakened by the memories of my fallen comrades who had not made it home. This was the beginning of my post-traumatic stress disorder (PTS), brought on by combat fatigue, an affliction not recognized back in 1969.

As I've related, I had a number of close calls in Nam, and it's a miracle I got out alive. But, for the rest of my life, I will be labeled with the stigma of "Vietnam Vet."

And, thoroughly traumatized by my experiences in Vietnam, I have, for the last forty years, wrestled with my conscience, with my morality, in having participated in "WAR."

Although I was home, I was there for only a short stay, as my military service wasn't finished. Still having six months left to serve in the Army, I was sent to Kaiserslautern, West Germany, where I would complete my overseas tour of duty as well as my military service. It sucked still being in the Army, and I wanted out. I'd had enough of this "theater," the theater of war.

I became the driver for the C.O., the Company Commander. In this assignment I was like a chauffeur, but it was good because my C.O. always had a three-day weekend; and, being his driver, I could get him to sign my weekend passes, thereby bypassing the First Sergeant, who ordinarily would have been the one to sign my passes. Once I had my pass, I would head over to the Air Force Terminal and check the flight manifest to see where flights were going. Having a Military Identification Card, I could hop on any plane with an empty seat and take a flight to anywhere. This way, I was able to travel to England, to Spain, to Rome, and to Greece. More often, though, I just took a train to Paris, my favorite place to hang out. I loved the art there, and spent most of my time in the city's museums.

The place to meet girls in Paris was the café scene: Led Zeppelin music ("Stairway to Heaven"), a bottle of wine, some cheese, some French bread. Picnicking along the Seine River, just below Notre Dame, where artists painted, made for romance, which was great because European attitudes about sex were freer than those in the United States. It was the sixties, the era of "Make Love, Not War."

One weekend I went to Amsterdam, capital of the Netherlands, and in a single day saw *Easy Rider* at the movies and caught a midnight live performance of the musical *Hair*. Among the coolest features of Amsterdam were the canals with the barges. There was also the Red Light District, which was fun to check out. Although I couldn't afford to "pay," walking along the streets and looking at the lingerie-clad women sitting in the windows was fun; you could window shop.

When catching the train back to Kaiserslautern, I always took the latest train possible that would still allow me to get back to base on time. This meant that I would have to sleep on the train, which was not easy. Always there was a social scene on the train, and it was easy to meet women traveling through Europe. Very tempting. Sometimes I would reach base late for Monday morning formation, and eventually this led to trouble. The First Sergeant became pissed off by my tardiness, particularly after he found out that I was usurping his authority by getting the C.O. to sign my weekend passes. After a few such incidents of lateness, he started plotting to get me.

One weekend, he placed me on guard duty in the mountains, patrolling a road that the military used for field exercises. The first time, all went normally. The next time, though, he got my Platoon Sergeant to ask for a ride downtown. Not thinking any thing about it, I agreed. On the way, the Platoon Sergeant, who was out of uniform and wearing civilian clothes, asked me to stop at a liquor store, where he picked up a bottle of beer. Getting back into the jeep, he opened the bottle and took a couple of swigs. As we drew closer to town, he asked me to drop him off at the Triangle, an area where no military personnel or vehicles were allowed. He pointed to a spot to drop him off, and I let him out. As he climbed out, however, he left the open bottle of beer in the jeep. And, no sooner had he shut the door than the MPs showed up, opened the door, and said, "You're in an off-limits area, soldier."

Then the MPs smelled the beer, and now I was really in deep shit because driving a military vehicle with an open container of alcohol in an off-limits area, while supposedly being on guard duty, is a court martial offense. In a time of war, you could be executed by firing squad for not being at your station.

70

They could have thrown me into the stockade, the military prison; and I could see where all this was headed. Confiscating my jeep, they called in some other MPs who had a vehicle, and I was escorted to their vehicle. Sitting there, I noticed that these MPs had 9th Infantry patches on their uniforms. I asked them when they had served in Vietnam, and it turned out that all of us had been there at the same time. We had been in Dong Dam at the same time, as well. So we shared stories.

On the way back to base, I asked them if they would turn me in to my C.O. instead of taking me to the stockade. They agreed, and my C.O. was awakened to come to his office and take custody of me. Arriving, he released the MPs, and told me to sit down and tell him what happened. I related my story, and he got the picture. Two things were in my favor. First, my C.O. was from Waverly, Virginia, where my grandparents lived, and he knew my family. We had already established this in earlier conversations; when driving him around, we would talk about the great fishing holes in the black water of Suffolk County. Second, he would be getting out of the Army in two weeks, as was I, and he didn't need the hassle of my situation so close to his departure.

This incident could have tarnished my military record, which, up to that time, I had managed to keep clean. Had the First Sergeant gotten his way, though, I would have received a Dishonorable Discharge. Ultimately, however, I exacted some measure of justice out of all of this. As it turned out, the First Sergeant was approaching the end of his 20-year Army career, and was about to retire, when he suddenly received orders to go to Vietnam for his last year of duty in the military. Was this a coincidence, or had he shot himself in the foot, so to speak, because the C.O. had learned of his plot against me? At any rate, as fate would have it, nothing came of the incident, and I was spared a Dishonorable Discharge.

Shortly thereafter, I was out of the service for good, glad to be free once again and back in the States. But there was just one problem: I was right back in same house as before, living with Dad and Rose again. And nothing had changed. It was still the same old bullshit: Dad still drinking, Rose still raging.

Rose and Hinton Harrison, Sr., and the author after returning home from Vietnam.

CHAPTER FIFTEEN
WAY OUT WEST

It didn't take long before I grew restless and needed to be alone. One day, while listening to the radio, I heard John Denver singing "Rocky Mountain High." That did it. With $100 in my pocket, a backpack, a few items of clothing, and my sleeping bag, I walked out the door and hit the road.

Hitchhiking westward across the United States, I never gave any thought to the possibility of danger, especially after what I had already been through. When I put my mind to do something, that's it. Each night, after a day of travel, I would find a tree to sleep under, outside of whatever town I was near. I would just go into the woods and camp. You might think this was crazy, not exactly Bible school summer camp, but it was a lot safer than Vietnam.

While in Nam, the magazine pictures of home that had made the greatest impression on me, and which I then held in my heart, were of the Rocky Mountains of Colorado; Sedona, Arizona; and Yosemite, California. And so I just kept on hitchhiking and walking until, eventually, I found my way to all three places, spending enough time in each to experience, for real, the travel fantasies that had kept me going in Vietnam.

This traveling was something that I just had to do in order to feel human again, and to try and regain some sense of personal pride in being free again. It is hard to describe what you wrestle with inside of your mind after you've been through war. Your life can never be the same again, and you don't take anything for granted anymore. I screwed up a few wonderful relationships because of my war-spawned restlessness. Once you get hyped up by war, something that war does to you, it's hard to settle down again. For me, as a result of this, drugs and alcohol became the crutches that destroyed everything that had meant anything to me.

73

Along the way on my trip west, I had some interesting adventures. My first ride was with a teenaged couple on their way to Kansas City. When they stopped and asked me where was I going, I said, "Anywhere west." I climbed in, the girl turned up the car radio, and we sped off down the highway. Leaning back in the seat and shutting my eyes, I fell asleep. After a short nap, I was awakened by a strange noise that sounded like a little motor pump running. Looking around, I realized that we had stopped at a gas station. The hood of the car was up, the trunk was open, and the boy was standing next to the car. The girl was in the station, talking to the attendant, being real friendly to him. Presently the pump sound stopped, the boy shut the trunk, walked to the front of the car, and shut the hood. Then he climbed into the car, the girl ran up and jumped into the front seat, and we took off down the road.

It turned out that they had siphoned gasoline out of the ground tank. As a diversion, the girl had kept the station attendant busy by flirting with him. She had asked the attendant if he ever got horny, sitting around the station all night by himself. She said that he couldn't keep his eyes off her tits. Then, sliding over to her boyfriend, she put her arm around him and offered him a bite of her candy bar. She kissed him on the neck, laughing as her head slid down onto his lap. I leaned back to catch some more shuteye. When I awakened, I found that we had stopped on the side of the road. The girl was looking in the rearview mirror, smoking a cigarette as she pulled her hair back into a ponytail. The boy said, "This is as far as we go before turning off." He told me that this was the best spot for hitching a ride; it would be easier for me to catch another ride here. And on that note, we parted ways.

Walking along the shoulder of the highway, I heard a car pull up behind me, followed by an amplified voice ordering me to stop where I was and not to move. It was a Highway Patrol officer, talking into a megaphone. Getting out of his car, his hand on his gun, he stood behind the open car door and asked me if I had any concealed weapons. When I answered that I didn't, he cautiously approached me.

"Where you traveling?"

"California eventually, I hope."

"Do you have any I.D. on you?"

After running a background check on me, he said that he had no reason to detain me. "Just keep on traveling. I don't want to see you around here again," he warned.

For a while, I stood on the side of the road in the noonday sun, then walked for a short distance, stopped, and leaned on my backpack. Presently, something off in the distance caught my attention. The shimmering heat mirage made it difficult to see and identify, but it looked like a dog walking parallel to the road. Just then a car pulled up on the shoulder just ahead of me and stopped. Walking up to the car, I opened the door and asked the driver how far he was going. He answered that he was headed to Boulder, Colorado, which was perfect because that was my first stop of interest on my journey west. As we drove off I could see, in the side rearview mirror, the Highway Patrol officer who had stopped me, pulled off on the side of the road, holding a rifle, and leaning over the hood of his car. It turned out that what I had taken to be a dog was actually a coyote; and the officer was taking shots at it.

Reaching Boulder, I got out of the car and thanked the driver, walked around the mall, then stopped to sit on a bench. A hippie-type girl walked up to me and asked me where was I from. Telling her I was from Baltimore, we talked for a while. She asked me if I wanted to hang out with her, and said I could leave my belongings at her house. Arriving there, she asked if I had a place to stay. When I told her I didn't, she invited me to crash there at her place for the night. This was cool and I really appreciated it. We hung out all day, hiked through the town of Nederland, and then returned to her place for dinner. She had a boyfriend who was cool with my crashing there for the night. They had some friends over for dinner who, it just turned out, were going to Telluride for a festival.

The next day we all headed into the Rockies, bound for Telluride, and the drive was beautiful. Everything I had dreamed about was really happening. When we reached Telluride, I found it breathtaking. Everyone was friendly, and the scent of patchouli oil hung in the air. A ticket for the festival fell into my hand, and I continued with the flow, hanging out for a few days. People were sharing, and everything I needed was taken care of. Life was sweet. Asking around if anyone was going to Sedona, Arizona, I met a couple of girls from Germany who were going that way, and they said they would welcome my company. So we hooked up, hung out, and looked around for anyone else bound for Sedona.

At the Festival, we met a Native American Hopi woman, Alisa, selling jewelry, who was going to the Hopi Reservation in Arizona. She offered us a ride to her village, and we accepted. After helping her pack up, we set off down the road. That evening we reached our destination, and could see that a large storm, threatening rain, was brewing. If you've ever visited the southwest, especially northern Arizona, during an electrical storm, you know that the weather can be intense.

Our new friend Alisa took us to a campsite located just where you entered the road to the Hopi Prophecy Rock overlooking a vista. This afforded us a great view of the storm off in the distance. Leaving us there, she said she would return in the morning. As the storm approached, we found ourselves wrapped in hair-raising white-light electrical energy flashes.

Later, Alisa decided to come back and retrieve us, inviting us to spend the night on the reservation in one of their family's guesthouses. So, grabbing our gear, we climbed into her car and headed to the guesthouse, which was not far down the road. Upon our arrival, she showed us around, and told us to make ourselves at home. Then we called it a night.

The next morning, Alisa showed up bright and early to invite us to her mother's house for breakfast. It turned out that her father, Thomas Banyacga, and her mother, Fermina, were Hopi Elders. After breakfast, we watched a documentary about the Hopi Prophecy, a very interesting piece about the Peabody Mining Company's exploitation of the uranium on the Hopi's land, and the effects this had on the indigenous Hopi people in the area.

Alisa took us to another part of the reservation called the Village of Oraibi. There, we entered a *Kiva*, a Hopi ceremonial chamber, and spent time with Grandfather David Monongya, one of the last true living Hopi leaders. Meeting him was truly a special opportunity. He was a blind, very frail, sweet elderly man, and we felt blessed to be in his presence. As we conversed, he described how Sedona was a sacred ceremonial place for the Hopi people; and he told us that we should visit there. At this we looked at each other knowingly, as Sedona was our next stop.

After the meeting, Alisa took us back to the trading post, where we hitched a ride to Flagstaff, then down to Sedona. Arriving, we set up camp out in the red rocks up towards Boynton Canyon. Once our camp was established, we began hiking, exploring Long Canyon. The next day we hiked to Cathedral Rock. A large heart-shaped rock, called the Temple of Light, is there, and you can watch great sunrises and sunsets from this spot. They say that this location is a vortex for star activation, because at night the view of the stars is spectacular.

Hiking back from Cathedral Rock, we met a guy who was going to Los Angeles. Hitching a ride with him, we talked him into stopping at Yosemite first. When we reached Yosemite, we set up camp in Sunnyside Walk-in. Yosemite is one of the most breathtaking places in California. The sunlight on Half Dome is a beautiful sight. By now I had connected with one of the German girls, and after sitting around the campfire, munching on some dry food, and sharing stories, the two of us cuddled up for the night. The next day, we hiked up from our camp into the clouds. Here it was too cold to hang out, as none of us had any warm clothes, so we returned and broke camp, then hit the road.

Reaching Los Angeles, we headed for Venice Beach, where we spent the night camping on the beach. By now, I was running out of money. The girls wanted to go to San Francisco, and I had to make a choice. I didn't know anyone in San Francisco, but I did have a friend in San Diego, Jerry Sheehan, who could help me out. So the girls and I went our separate ways, the girls to San Francisco and I to San Diego.

Making it to San Diego, I contacted Jerry, an old friend I had grown up with in Baltimore. Now living in San Diego, he worked at the San Diego Ship Yard. We got together and he let me hang out at his place. This actually turned out to be the right decision because he was doing some landscaping on his yard, and he offered to pay me to help out. So I jumped in to help, and he paid me enough to buy a plane ticket back to Baltimore. During my stay in San Diego, I met some of his friends, and we did some partying. I even got in some surfing. Then it was time for me to head back to the East Coast.

CHAPTER SIXTEEN
STREET CORNER MIME

Upon my return to Baltimore, I discovered that I was eligible for college under the GI Bill. So I registered in Community College, Baltimore, Maryland, with a major in Psychology. While reading the textbook for the course Psych 101, however, I was dismayed to find that the profile for "Dysfunctional" could have been a perfect description of me. This so upset me that I closed the book, said goodbye to Psychology, and changed my major to the Art and Theater Program.

My acting teacher thought I was a good mime, and recommended me to Tony Montanaro in South Paris, Maine. Watching Tony perform at the Townsend State Teachers College, I was impressed, and I filled out an application for Celebration Mime Theater. I was accepted, and headed off to Maine to study and perform mime from 1972 to 1975.

Maine is a beautiful state. During my time there in the early 1970s, the population of the whole state was less than one million. I suppose one reason for such a low population was that there were few jobs to be had there at that time. However, I managed to find a job at the Milner Wood Products factory, working on the timber-cutting table as 30-foot-long green wood boards, wet and heavy with sap, dropped onto a stacking table. The labor was intensive.

I lived at Celebration Mime Theater, in exchange for which I helped Tony convert the barn there into a theater. We also turned the horse stalls into student dorms, as we were located some distance from the closest town, South Paris, which had no hotels anyway. Purchasing a teepee from nomadic makers in Oregon, I set it up close to the Theater as a place for me to live. However, the Maine winters were so bone-chillingly cold that I soon had had enough of the teepee-living scene, and headed to Portland, Maine.

In Portland, I performed around town in Old Town, calling my act "Street Corner Mime." I also performed with the Children's Theater of Maine in Portland, touring the State of Maine while attending the University of Maine, Portland, and Gorham.

While in Mime School at the Celebration Mime Theater, I had filled out an application for Clown College, mailed it off, and forgot about it. A year later, while sitting in one of my college classes, I heard my name called over the intercom, and I was told to report to the Dean's Office. I couldn't imagine why the Dean wanted to see me. When I arrived, he asked me to have a seat, then said, "I have Dean Bill Ballentine on the phone from Clown College in Venice Beach, Florida. He wants me to tell you that you have been accepted to attend the Ringling Brothers and Barnum and Bailey Circus Clown College."

CHAPTER SEVENTEEN
SEND IN THE CLOWN

In order to both raise some traveling money for my trip to Florida and to say goodbye to everyone, I decided to put on a farewell performance of "Street Corner Mime." I was about to leave behind everything that I had worked so hard to establish in Portland to go on another adventure. Maine had been good to me. I had even connected with my half-sister, Martha Gayle, there. A few years older than me, she was the daughter of a different father. Martha lived in Port Clyde, Maine, on Tenants Harbor. When I visited her house to meet her for the first time since we were babies, I learned that she had been adopted while I had gone on a wild ride with Dad. But one of the most interesting things that Martha and I had in common was that she had a red 1964 Ford Mustang fastback just like mine — same model, same color.

Clown College was the most fun school I have ever attended. The student body comprised 50 performing artists, selected out of 1,500 applicants, the most energetic group of young people you could imagine. We launched into a program that taught us everything about clowning: Make-up, magic, prop building, dance, mime, slapstick, pratfalls, juggling, unicycling, tightrope walking, stilt walking, trapeze, and the history of clowning. There was also a library of films about circus performances and the history of the circus. The experience and knowledge I gained were priceless.

After we completed the program, 20 of us were selected to become clowns. Those selected had to be consistently high-energy, hyperactive types because the life of a circus clown entailed performing two shows daily during weekdays, and three daily on weekends. On your day off, you traveled with the circus to the next performance destination. After graduation, we each received our Clown College certificate and a red nose. Now that we were officially clowns, we were invited to meet Ervin Feld and his son, Kenneth Feld, in their office. The elder Feld was a very thin, frail old man. Seated in a big leather chair, wearing Coke-bottle glasses, he was smoking a big cigar. They asked me to have a seat. Congratulating me for completing the Clown College program, they asked me if I would like to be a clown for the Ringling Bros. and Barnum & Bailey Circus. Of course I said "Yes." Why not? What the hell? It sounded like a great adventure, and I had nothing else to do anyway.

Before hitting the road, we spent about three weeks rehearsing for the show in Venice, Florida, the winter headquarters of the circus. There were two shows, or units, that traveled across the country at the same time — the Blue Unit and the Red Unit. I was in the Blue Unit.

After our rehearsals in Venice, we hit the road, and for the next year I lived on the circus train, along with the animals and all of my fellow performers. I traveled with the circus across the country, stopping in every major city in the U.S., performing in coliseums and sports arenas in front of audiences of as many as 60,000 people.

The most incredible moment in my performing career was the first time I stepped into center ring in the spotlight for the first time, and looked at the sea of faces watching my every move. I spotted a boy far up in the bleacher seats, standing and waving, and yelling, "Clown!" To be sure he was waving at me, I waved back at him with both hands. He waved back with both hands. I did a jig. He did a jig. It was a very personal moment that reminded me of my childhood days on the street corner under the streetlight. I will always treasure the feeling that welled up in my heart. I felt pure innocent love. It was as though I was standing in celestial light.

I have always wanted to do a story about what goes on backstage with the clowns. I would call it "Clown Alley," and it would be a great stage piece giving a look behind the scenes of the "Greatest Show on Earth." There are some interesting stories to be told about the life of a circus clown on the road.

I did learn one important fact about the circus: If you don't like the smell of shit, and especially of tiger piss, then the circus life is not for you. Let me share a story about tigers. They would always be lined up in their cages backstage; and, if you weren't paying attention when walking by the cages, they would piss on you. The piss-squirting distance of the female tigers was a good 10 feet. So whenever you saw their tails go straight, a sign that they were about to unload, you knew that you had better not be within their range.

The circus was an exciting adventure and a lot of fun. However, I came to have issues with the abuse of the circus animals — how they would be caged up for long periods in confined spaces. And worse, as in the case of a female elephant named Annabel.

In each show, Annabel and I would be the first to walk out during the all-cast walk-around that signaled the start of the show. One evening, I came up to her and began scratching and petting her behind the ears; elephants love to get scratched behind the ears. She brought her trunk around, sniffing; and, once she sensed my presence and recognized me, I hugged her trunk and pretended to blow into her trunk like it was a trumpet. I said to her, "Annabel, I love you." This was a regular ritual between us. Looking into her eyes this time though, I immediately noticed that she was crying. Looking closely at the bone under one of her eyes, I saw that she had an open wound. Earlier, I had noticed the animal assistant using his claw hook stick, used to poke the elephants in order to get them moving, on Annabel. I saw this guy being abusive, hooking the stick in the bone socket of her now injured eye, trying to force her head down. However, I hadn't realized the damage he had done until now. The hook had torn the skin right under her eye. Having some major issues about abuse myself, this, needless to say, opened some old and painful wounds for me, and it made me sick. I was not a happy clown. And, shortly thereafter, I said goodbye to the circus.

CHAPTER EIGHTEEN
CITY BY THE BAY

My circus days behind me, I decided to hitchhike from Seattle to San Francisco. On the way, while leaving Ashland, Oregon, I became stranded in the mountains during a snowstorm. The car I was riding in had no snow chains; and, as a result, going up a mountain, we started skidding off the road and got stuck. Tractor-trailer trucks had jack-knifed across the highway, blocking the lanes and bringing traffic to a complete standstill; no one was going anywhere. Stranded, we found ourselves in a whiteout snow, a blizzard. Not being dressed for cold weather, I had a rough night. As luck would have it, though, the woman in the car in front of us lived just off the next exit. Her house was close enough for us to reach it by foot, and she invited us to spend the night.

By the next day, the road had been cleared, and we continued on. Finally, we entered California and warmer weather. Just outside of Sacramento, the driver with whom I had hitched the ride dropped me off. At a hamburger joint, I performed some juggling for a hamburger and French fries.

Sitting on the railing of a bridge, eating my food, I noticed a boat on the bank of the Sacramento River. It was an old wooden boat, about 8 feet long. And it was then that an idea hit me: What an adventure it would be to float down the Sacramento River on that boat!

Entering a nearby bait and tackle store, I asked the man behind the counter if he knew who owned the boat, and I told him that I wanted to buy it. As it turned out, the boat was his. Explaining what I wanted to do with it, I asked him if he would sell it to me. He agreed, and sold it to me for $5.00.

Needed a paddle, I broke a board in half, and it split at an angle — thin at one end, wide at the other. Perfect. Throwing my backpack in, I jumped into the boat, shoved off from shore, — and down the river I began to float. ("Row, row, row your boat, gently down the stream. Merrily, merrily, merrily, merrily, Life is but a dream.")

Along the riverbanks, I found plenty to snack on. The land was all farmland, and fruit and nuts had fallen from the trees onto the ground. I would stop at night, find a dry spot along the riverbank, start a campfire, kick back, and listen to the river rushing by. Watching the night sky, I wished upon the occasional shooting star.

As I neared San Francisco, I pulled the boat up onto dry land, found my way to the freeway, and hitched a ride on the back of a motorcycle across the Golden Gate Bridge and into the city. It was a beautiful sunny day when I arrived. Heading to Haight Ashbury, I found a kind brother with whom I shared a toke, and then went into Golden Gate Park. That first night I slept in the park under a tree. The fragrant smell of the eucalyptus trees surrounding me hung in the air. The next morning I headed to the house of a mime friend, Antoinette Atell, whom I had met when I had been in town with the circus. She had come backstage to Clown Alley to meet the clowns, and we became friends. Hanging out together, she had shown me around the city before the circus departed.

Appearing on her doorstep, I told her that I had fallen madly in love with San Francisco, and that I had decided to live in the city. I asked her if she could put me up until I found a place to live, and she received me with open arms. We did a few gigs together, and she gave me one of her gigs, a New Year's Eve Party at the home of Thomas and Margery Leighton, two famous painters. Just before midnight, however, Thomas passed away. But, just as in the circus when they would call in the clowns, "The show must go on," so I performed anyway.

At midnight bagpipes rang in the new year of 1977. At this party, I made acquaintances that still last to this day. These contacts led to additional engagements, which launched a great performance adventure for me in San Francisco. After a few gigs, I found my own place to live, on Union Street. Then I started miming in the streets of downtown San Francisco, at the corner of Stockton and Geary in Union Square. The city adopted me, and my career took off.

Margery Leighton became a close friend, and I actually modeled for the students in her painting class. She painted me in my mime outfit, a sweet image that would eventually be donated to the Shriners Hospital for Children. At the New Year's Eve party, I also met Rick and Mary Jo Rodriquez, and still stay in touch with them. Rick is a painter who teaches at City College in the Art Department. I was there when their two boys, Theo and Dante, were born, and watched them grow up.

Bill and Lynn Twist became good friends after Lynn had hired me for an annual street party she had organized. I have been around long enough to see their kids, Billy, Zack, and Summer, grow up as well. Lynn Twist's name may sound familiar; she was a fundraiser for the Hunger Project, and authored a book titled, *The Soul of Money*.

The romance of my life happened in San Francisco. However, given my history with relationships, coupled with my own fears of rejection, I fled from this romance, from love, despite the heartbreaking separation from the feelings of joy and pleasure. I chose the depression that followed, holding onto only the fond memories.

Mayor George Moscone and I became close friends, and we often participated together in fun public events. Seeing me performing on the street, Mayor Moscone would pull up in his chauffeured limousine, lower the window, stick his head out, and say something along the lines of, "Would you join me for a kid's event in Golden Gate Park?" We would then cruise over to entertain the children in our own special way. We appeared in an ad campaign together to clean up the city: "Beautify San Francisco." In the campaign I held a broom with a happy face on it, sweeping the city's streets. I still have that picture, autographed by Mayor Moscone.

Sadly, after Mayor Moscone was shot and killed in 1978, San Francisco changed. As a result, I eventually decided to move on; but I truly left my heart in San Francisco. Here is the poem I composed upon my departure from the City by the Bay:

> You harbored my soul, a friend you were, when I was all alone, San Francisco, beautiful City by the Bay, you filled my loneliness, and lifted my spirits, you let me express my innermost feelings, your beauty sparked my imagination, now sitting here not knowing, which way to go, let me set sail, you have my heart, I lost a friend to despair, a shot heard around the world, now his soul rests in peace, a friendship I will treasure, as I explore the world.

The author and Mayor George Moscone in San
Francisco.

Painting of the author by Margery Lester Leighton.

CHAPTER NINETEEN
MUGGED

One day, while I was still in San Francisco, doing a commercial film shot on top of a cable car for KFRC Radio, a man named Burton Goldberg, jogging up Powell and Lombard Streets, stopped and introduced himself. He then invited me to perform in Florida at Coconut Grove at the Mutiny, a playhouse for the decadent and flamboyant party-hard wealthy jet set.

I accepted, and in the ensuing relationship I learned a lot about myself, learned that I was always attracting abusive people into my life. About this let me just say that I experienced both good and bad times during this gig. But it did open doors that led to my spending many years in Florida — touring, performing, and appearing on *Skipper Chuck*, *Duck Duck Goose*, and *Small Wonders*, as well as at special events as far south as Key West at the Pier House. Through the Michelle Pommier Agency, I found additional work in modeling, fashion, print, and commercials, as well as in film.

It was while in Florida that I had the dream about my real mother, which I've described earlier: The dream that jarred me awake one night, my inner child's voice crying for Mommy. At that time, I didn't know where she lived. Later, when I learned she was living in Pointe Vedra Beach, Florida, it struck me how near I had been to her for so long and didn't even know it.

I was in Miami during the riots. One evening I took a bus, intending to go out to dinner at Coconut Grove. Unfortunately, I got off at the wrong bus stop. As I waited for another bus, five young black men approached me. Before I knew what was happening, they had struck me a number of times on the head with a broken piece of concrete, knocking me to the ground. As I lay there, my soul actually left my body, and I hovered overhead, watching my attackers continue to beat me.

This may sound strange, but during this experience a bright angelic light form appeared next to me. It seemed to be inviting me to come with it. I thought, "I am not ready to go yet." With that, my soul returned to my body in a flash, and I somehow struggled to my feet. By then my attackers had fled and the police had shown up. Looking at some mug shots, I was able to identify one of my attackers. He had a record and the police picked him up.

At times I have lost my motivation, having suffered through the years from serious bouts of depression, even to the point of considering suicide. It seems like all the abuse I have suffered in my life — the mugging and everything else — has caught up with me. From that moment in time on the street corner of Main and Grand in Coconut Grove, where I was mugged, I have at times spiraled downward into my own cave of despair, losing hope. I sometimes feel as though everything is slowly slipping away, even my will to live. A person can take only so much.

CHAPTER TWENTY
LESSONS ON DIVISION

After the mugging, which was yet another humiliating lesson in shattered faith in the kindness of human beings, I met a genuinely kind and gentle man named George Durst. One night, after my performance at the Mutiny, he invited me to Montreal, Canada, to perform at *La Sarrs* ("The Green House"), a restaurant that he owned in Old Montreal. It turned out that Montreal held an interesting lesson of its own: The city is divided into French-speaking and English-speaking areas. There is a struggle among the people of Quebec over whether French or English should be the official language of the province. This creates tension, and I sensed that you had to take one side or the other, that neutrality wasn't an option. When I was not performing in the restaurant, I would go into the streets of Old Town, Montreal, in the evenings and perform. Old Town was an exciting area in which to perform.

While in Montreal, I did a commercial for Coca-Cola in which they blocked off a street and set up a 50-foot-long table, filled with food, for a block party feast. In the commercial I rode my unicycle, with a kid on my shoulder, down the entire length of the table. The scene ended with the kid and me sitting at the end of the table, drinking Cokes. Also, during this time, one of my favorite rock groups was Super Tramp, and a local radio station hired me to be their mascot. In this role I would appear on stage as Super Tramp came on to play. This was a highlight of my stay in Montreal.

Returning to Miami, I hooked up with Howard Schwartz Promotions. Howard was staging Disco Events, in partnership with Denny Terro of Dance Fever, on a Florida tour; this was a Merv Griffin Production. We really had a good time on this event, touring around Florida, doing the Disco scene. After the tour was over, Howard sent a group of dance competition winners and me to South America — Caracas, Venezuela, and Geto, Ecuador — to perform at discos there.

This was back in 1983; and while in Caracas, I was often approached by people because I was an American. They would express their criticisms of the U.S., suggesting that our nation had an imperialist government. They pontificated their idea of a popular revolution in which they would invade the U.S., creating a shift in power. I pointed out that I was the Peace Clown, not a politician, and was there simply to entertain. But I cannot imagine that anyone would want less than they have, for life is truly a precious commodity that, protected by the principles of a free society, is protected by an organized system for their safety, happiness, and future security. Anyone considering changing things had better be able to promise the people a more secure future, because war really sucks. To think that we still fight in "wars." What a fucked-up condition human nature has gotten us into.

And here it is now, the year 2007 as I write this, with the daily news headlines proclaiming that immigration at all borders is the central issue of concern. What do people really want? Why is it so difficult to provide the basic needs — food, shelter, and health care? The amount of money spent on war is so insane, especially when people are starving and a fucking bullet costs more than feeding a life.

After returning from South America, I discovered that Six Flags in Baltimore, at the Inner Harbor, was looking for clowns. So I auditioned for the job and was hired, and Six Flags paid very well.

The accountant at Six Flags was an African-American woman, who gave me my paycheck twice a month. She became my next heart-wrenching affair, one that taught me important lessons about a dark side of human nature: Racism. I really enjoyed her company, but just going to her neighborhood to pick

94

her up for a date was life-threatening; the stark memories of my mugging in Miami made me extra cautious. Also, the things that people, both white and black, expressed about the inherent differences between the races, and the superiority of one race or the other, were challenging to deal with rationally.

Our relationship finally came to a close when my job at Six Flags ended, and she announced that she was returning to college.

CHAPTER TWENTY-ONE
THE BIG APPLE

My friend Jean Doswell in New York City called and talked me into going to the city. With my job at Six Flags over and my accountant friend returning to college, I thought, "Why not?" Taking a train to the Big Apple, I decided to hang out there for a while. New York City sounded like it offered great new networking opportunities. Jean is married to John Doswell, of Doswell Productions in Manhattan. We had met back in the 1970s in San Francisco at a conference they had produced, a multimedia presentation for IBM. At the time I had been hired by IBM to perform mime, and the Doswells and I have been friends ever since.

During the time I was in New York City, the Doswells lived on 47th and 8th Avenue. As things turned out, I didn't get much work to speak of in the city, but it was great fun hanging out with Jean and John. I would walk their daughter, Jhoneen, to her ballet class at Carnegie Hall, wait until her class was over, and then walk her back home. One Sunday morning, we were walking in Central Park, and for some reason Jhoneen just took off, running into the crowd and vanishing — every parent's worst nightmare. I just trusted that I was going to find her once she realized she had lost sight of me. Eventually she stopped and stood still. A woman standing next to her lifted and held her up so she would be visible above the crowd. Seeing Jhoneen, I ran up and retrieved her, and never let go of her hand again.

Jean and John had a sailboat docked at the 21st Street Pier, and, when I visited them, I would stay on the boat. The vantage point of the Hudson River afforded a great way to see New York City, with beautiful sunrises over the tower landscape of high rises. In the evening, you could kick back on a big couch at the end of the pier and take in the sunsets, watching the sun descend behind New Jersey.

During my stay in New York City, the city finally held a belated welcome-home ticker tape parade for Vietnam veterans. I participated in this historical event by riding my unicycle in the parade.

CHAPTER TWENTY-TWO
I VISIT DAD

Following the parade, I decided to go to Baltimore to see one of my best friends, Bob Revere, and his wife, Laura, both schoolteachers. "Mr. Bob," as he is known to his students, created a learning center program for Head Start that has received national attention. I have known Bob since elementary school, and we still stay in touch via e-mail.

While in Baltimore, I visited Dad, who by then was suffering from serious health problems. Rose was still there, being there for him "through hell and high water," as Dad would say. While visiting them at the old house, I found it uncomfortable to be there. So many haunting memories. But Dad and Rose were too old for me to bring up old issues, old wounds. If only Rose had told me that she was sorry for being so cruel to me. But neither she nor Dad ever apologized to me. It was always, "You deserved it."

So I will save it all for therapy. It's all a mystery to me, knowing the history of their relationship; it blows my mind. Just sitting in their presence brought up disturbing images of past unpleasantries that had happened right where I was sitting. How could Rose have put up with so much abuse and violence from Dad all these years? And now here she was taking care of him like he was a helpless little baby. As ill as Dad was, at times he was still belligerent and demanding, and he still controlled their relationship. I am not criticizing him. He harbored so much anger and fear that he was crippled emotionally. As a result, he would quickly turn defensive, erupting and lashing out in self-defense, to compensate for and conceal his low self-esteem.

Dad had always been defiant: "Don't tell me what to do!" If you suggested that he get help for his drinking problem he would yell, "I'll God damn do as I please and drink as much as I want!" as he drank Jack Daniels Whiskey straight from the bottle, slobbering as he slurred. The manufacturers of alcoholic beverages should be proud of Dad; he drank enough liquor, all by himself, to make them rich. Finally, he would pass out on the floor, lying in his own vomit. I would clean up the mess and try to get him to bed. The next day, I would be walking on eggs, not knowing what he might do next.

But now, by his side, I took Dad's hand in mine for the first time. He used to grab my hand in a strong, vice-like handshake and wouldn't let go. But now he no longer had the strength to do that, his grip feeble. Holding his hand gently, I looked him in the eye. Looking back into my eyes, he could tell that I had seen the Dark Side, and he closed his eyes as if to block out this revelation. I massaged his hands, his arms, his neck, his head. I lay down next to him, hugging him. I could feel him feebly resisting my affection. For him to surrender to my affection would have been a sign, an admission, of weakness — something to be avoided at all costs. And so, Dad would take his pain to the grave with him.

CHAPTER TWENTY-THREE
ANAM CHARA

In stark contrast to Dad and Rose, I cannot help but think of my dear friend, Peggy Tolman Quinn, who lives in Boulder, Colorado, and whom I always stop and visit whenever I'm in the area. In all the years I have known Peggy; I have never heard her raise her voice or seen her get angry. She is always so patient, so tolerant, so compassionate.

Peggy created a Hospice to assist terminally ill people in their passage to the afterlife, calling her Hospice Anam Chara. In the days of the Celts, the *Anam Chara*, a Gaelic term meaning "soul friend," was an active and vital member of every village, who assisted the villagers with birth and dying. The Anam Charas were wise soul women who, along with loved ones, were present with those giving birth or those dying, celebrating the great mysteries of birth and death with chants and expressions of loving affection during life's transitions.

Peggy's quest to create such a place in the 21st Century in Boulder has been a dream come true. Like so many other visionaries, Peggy had awakened one morning — and it was then that, as though from deep within her cellular memory, came the call that the time had come for her to establish Anam Chara. A preset moment in time had arrived, and a pre-encoded signal was activated that took precedence over all of her other indoctrinations, obligations, and goals. For her to resist these forces would have led to a mental catastrophe.

Peggy calls it her "breakthrough." After 21 years of marriage and three beautiful children, the stress of being a wife, mother, and friend had consumed her. She had fulfilled her parental and societal obligations; success was not important anymore. But then her mother, her godmother, and her 29-year-old brother-in-law all died within the space of a few years.

Moreover, her youngest son developed cancer; and her daughter was in an accident that almost took her life.

In the midst of her grief and shock, Peggy lost her will to live; she felt as if she wanted to leave this world. However, a spiritual knowing deep inside of her pulled her out of her depression and into her true destiny and purpose. No more daydreaming. She heard the call of her calling, and a feeling of independence overwhelmed her. She moved forward through her own rite of passage into a place of trust.

It was 1987, a harmonic convergence year, and the International Conference on Dying, Death and Healing was scheduled to be held on the Island of Iona in Northern Scotland. Peggy knew she just had to go there and attend the conference. But how? Family obligations and financial debt were consuming her, and it seemed to her that her life was coming apart. Thus, to take time off from work and travel to Scotland seemed impossible.

It was then that Eleanor Detiger, a wealthy woman committed to making a difference in the world, called Peggy. Eleanor offered to pay for Peggy's trip to Iona, and from that point everything began to fall into place. Following her inner "knowing," Peggy took a leave of absence from work, and soon found herself (and "found herself") at the conference.

There, Peggy began to network, meeting many incredible people involved in changing the world's consciousness about death. One of the key people she met was Elisabeth Kubler-Ross, who would later take Peggy under her tax-exempt umbrella until Peggy was able to create her own non-profit organization and begin to fulfill her dream.

Peggy was elated. On September 29, 1987, the Feast Day of the Archangel Michael, bringer of light and courage, slayer of dragons, and her own mythical hero, Peggy gazed out over the North Atlantic Ocean. In this moment of gratitude, she thought of her two Irish pioneer grandmothers, Maggie and Margaret, who followed their inner callings as young, courageous women.

Maggie made that desperate journey across the American Great Plains, in a covered wagon, into the Wild West of Wyoming. Homesteading there, she raised seven children, and lived to see a man walk on the Moon.

Margaret crossed the Atlantic Ocean as a teenaged girl, leaving behind her beloved Ireland to immigrate to America, and never again saw her parents or her homeland. Margaret also raised seven children. Impoverished in a material sense, she was rich with an abundance of love.

Like her grandmothers, Peggy also felt like a pioneer about to embrace her calling: To help people by creating a supportive living environment in times of life's transitions.

At this moment in her revelation, an elderly man, Mr. Troub, approached her and gave her *Traditions of Celtic People*, a book containing the first written versions of ancient oral Celtic traditions. Mr. Troub was the son of a historian whose own father had written the book. He said to Peggy, "The work you are interested in doing is a contemporary application of the ancient traditions of Celtic wisdom — *Anam Chara* ('Soul Friend')." On this beautiful sunny day, walking in grace in this sacred place, on this sacred ground, of her ancestors, Peggy Tolman Quinn's vision came into focus.

Although religiosity was not for Peggy, in this perfect moment she completely felt the spiritual energy. Purple heather flowers were in full bloom. On this warm, sweet day, a soft breeze caressing her being, she suddenly embodied all that exists. She began to imagine herself being the Little Prince on his isle of fire, keeping the moment pure.

Looking around, she took in the grazing sheep, snow-white from the moisture of the misty morning, and the emerald-green fields, as she breathed deeply of the culture of this magical land. Inspired, in-spirit between the invisible realm and the physical world, she was one with the Mist of Iona, one with nature, one with All. Bowing her head in a moment of meditation, she noticed a heather root, in the shape of a dragon, lying on the ground. Reaching down, she grasped this precious totem gift from Spirit. She held it in her palms, as though it encompassed her dream. Her memories of her connection to this land, to this time, to this place are in her heart for eternity.

Dragon protection. Seeing her destiny, she embraced it with love and devotion. Her heart was filled with the magic of the experience at this never-ending threshold. Continually, it would enlarge and forever change her life. As Thomas Moore observed, "For there are places in this world that are neither here nor there, neither up nor down, neither real nor imaginary . . ."

Returning to the U.S., Peggy established her first Anam Chara Hospice in Denver, Colorado, creating a home to comfort and heal those going through life's transitions. Later, she established her second Anam Chara in Boulder. Ultimately, there will be an Anam Chara in every neighborhood where people feel called upon to live in community, in remembrance of who we are.

Anam Charas are unique, holistic, neighborhood residences where elder care provides the matrix of community living. They provide an intimate, nurturing environment in which the dignity and respect of each resident is celebrated, with family, staff, and volunteers finding support for their personal growth and life passages.

CHAPTER TWENTY-FOUR
ROCKY MOUNTAIN HIGH

I was back in Miami performing for Howard Schwartz Productions when Burton Goldberg called to see if I wanted to perform for a grand opening of a new restaurant in Aspen, Colorado, of which he was part owner. Taking him up on this offer, I met him in Philadelphia, at a dentist's office. Burton had his own plane, and we flew to Aspen. The gig didn't work out, however, as there was some conflict over the restaurant's ownership, so I started performing in the streets of Aspen.

Peter McMann, of the Marketing Department at Highlands Ski Company, approached me with a deal to be the company's mascot. He offered me housing, a weekly salary, and all the skiing I could ever dream of doing, so I jumped at the opportunity and skied all winter.

I soon become a resident of Aspen, working with Marcus Morton Promotions, performing at parties and special events, traveling around Colorado ski resorts: Telluride, Beaver Creek, Steam Boat, Breckenridge, and Vail. I met Jon Barnes, the genius behind the *Ultimate Taxi*; and we teamed up to document his performances, working together on this for the next 10 years. Jon, his wife Beth, and I became good friends, and I witnessed two of his children come into the world; believe it or not, both children were boys with red hair. Once, when I pointed out to the boys how lucky they were to have Beth and Jon as parents, Beth asked, "What do you know about parenting or raising children?" I responded that I knew good parents when I saw them.

I had the great opportunity to appear in John Denver's *Rocky Mountain High* show; and I was also in a commercial with John for the Aspen Hospital. I got the lead in a Reunite Wine commercial, juggling three bottles of wine, which was shot in Aspen for national TV during Super Bowl XIII. I even produced and performed in 50 episodes of my own weekly TV show, *Life Styles of the Poor and Unknown*, broadcast on local Grassroots Television in Aspen. My show was an interview program featuring local characters and interesting people.

CHAPTER TWENTY-FIVE
PEACE CLOWN MARCHING

Unfortunately, as luck would have it, I blew out my right knee during an aerobic marathon. As a result, I had to undergo surgery, which put me out of commission for a while. While recuperating, I was visited by some peace marchers, and I decided to join in their upcoming Peace March from Los Angeles to Washington, DC, a 1986 protest against global nuclear proliferation.

Having always been fascinated by migration, by human dynamics, and by in-group situations, I knew the Peace March would be a perfect opportunity to become a part of a large and diverse group of people. And so, following my recuperation, I set out on a pilgrimage, on foot, across the United States. Let me share with you one amusing memory of the March.

The Peace March was supported by donations from outside organizations, which often sent representatives to walk with the marchers along a portion of the route. These people came from different peace organizations. Sometimes, just your average citizen who wanted peace joined in as well. Church congregations and private-citizen groups from around the nation and the world also joined the March along the way. All of the marchers, whether representatives of some organization, church, or group, or whether average citizens, brought with them their respective concepts of peace, which differed, often significantly.

One group in particular, a brotherhood of monks, wore one-piece cloths they designed to make clothing choices less complicated. Simple in use, the garment could be worn in many ways. In the hot summer, the monks wore the cloth as a wraparound, or skirt, which could be perceived as a dress. The members of one of the more conservative groups in the march took offense at the dress-like configuration of this outfit, and expressed their displeasure.

We were about to enter Grand Island, Nebraska, one hot and humid summer morning. As we stood in line for breakfast at the mobile food kitchen, someone noticed a message posted on the information board and read it aloud. It said, "There will be a dress code today for the Peace Rally into Grand Island." Obviously some self-appointed authority from the conservative group, upset over the monks' outfits, took the initiative to put up this message for everyone to read.

In response, some of the marchers decided to obey this "Dress Code" quite literally, so they headed to the local thrift store and purchased dresses to wear. The result was quite a fanciful parade into town that day, and I will never forget the impression this made on me. I found it rather amusing to see the human spirit express itself so freely. Also about this time, Baba Ram Dass, author of the classic book, *Be Here Now*, joined the March, walking with us for a few days. I had the great opportunity to just "Be Here Now" with him, as we walked together along the trail to the peace we hoped to achieve in 1986.

And now here we are, more than 20 years later as I write this, with our leader fighting a personal war in the desert called: Peace?

Another memory from the Peace March: While passing through Baltimore, I met Pete Seeger. Hanging out on a street corner, we got caught up in a conversation about peace and freedom, enjoying each other's company in a sense of harmony. During our time together in this harmonious state of mind, we were free from such onerous intrusions as oppressive thoughts about nuclear threats and emotional tyranny. We became so lost in the moment, in fact, that we found ourselves left behind by the Peace March, and had to hitch a ride to catch up. Pete invited me to come sailing with him on his boat, *Freedom*, up on the Hudson River off Manhattan in New York. I've yet to take him up on his invitation.

CHAPTER TWENTY-SIX
OJAI

After the Peace March concluded in Washington, DC, I headed to Los Angeles in order to follow up on some contacts I had made during the March. One in particular was Fred Siegel, of Fred Siegel's, in Santa Monica, California. Fred hired me to perform on weekends in the shopping mall as a clown for kids, and the gig lasted through the summer. At this time, I decided to move to and live in Ojai, a small California community north of Los Angeles. In Ojai I found performance gigs in schools and at community events. J. Krishnamurti, who had also lived in Ojai, said something reflecting human problems that I find profound:

> Truth is a pathless land. Man cannot come to it through any organization, through any creed, through any dogma, priest or ritual, not through any philosophic knowledge or psychological technique. He has to find it through the understanding of the contents of his own mind, through observation and not through intellectual analysis or introspective dissection. Man has built in himself a fence of security — religious, political, personal. These manifest as symbols, ideas, and beliefs. The burden of these images dominates Man's thinking, his relationships and his daily life. These images are the cause of our problems, for they divide man from man.

Today, now that I am back living in the area, I make it a point to visit Ojai often, when I want to get away from Los Angeles. In Ojai I like to visit Pierre Grimes, a philosophy teacher, who has taught the "Spiritual Significance of the Platonic Dialectic," a classical Hellenic philosophy that influenced and enlightened many cultures of its time. I have taken a few of his classes, and they have inspired some thoughts of my own, such as "Plato in Ojai":

Plato thought of himself as a mere man of words; he inspired free thinking and insight into spirituality. To him, truth and wisdom in temperance was the path to a wholesome, just spirit. Plato was a real lover of knowledge, not content to abide by the multitude of opinions and trivial beliefs. He was all about freeing oneself to shine brightly with all that is. If Plato were alive today he would live in Ojai Valley with brilliant light beings.

While I was in Ojai, Stars Talent Agency in San Francisco was still representing me. They would call me once in a while, and I would drive to San Francisco to perform. Eventually, I established enough gigs in Los Angeles and San Francisco, and locations in between, to keep me busy.

Howard Schwartz, the promoter and special events producer whom I had worked for in Miami, was in Century City one weekend, staging an aerobic marathon competition, as I was just finishing a birthday party gig. Stopping by to see what Howard was up to, I stuck around for a while and helped out at the event. When it was over, he asked me what he could do for me.

As it so happened, a harmonic convergence happening was scheduled for August 16, 1987, in Teotihuacán, Mexico, on the Pyramid of the Sun. I expressed to Howard my desire to attend this event, and he gave me the necessary plane ticket. By the next day, at sunrise, I was sitting atop the Sun Temple in Teotihuacán, with a number of other people from around the world in ceremony. As I sat, I had a vision of Quetzalcoatl, the Bird Serpent Wisdom-Keeper, who appeared out of the sunrise and flew into my mind's eye. My imagination may have created this vision, but it was beautiful.

Returning to Ojai, I performed at parties in Los Angeles, and made trips to San Francisco for gigs there as well. After doing an industrial commercial for Hewlett-Packard, through Stars Talent Agency, I set out on the return trip home. Driving through Carmel, my Volkswagen van broke down at Rio and Highway 1, the Crossroads. And here I found myself in one of the most beautiful places in Central California: Carmel by the Sea, famous for its spectacular coastal location, as well as for its mayor, Clint Eastwood.

CHAPTER TWENTY-SEVEN
THE HILL OF THE HAWK

Taking advantage of the situation while my van was being repaired, I stopped in Esalen. And it was there that I met an incredible lady named Claire Chappellet, who lived in Big Sur. If the name sounds familiar, it's because her brother runs Chappellet Wines in the Sonoma wine country. The year was 1988, and I will never forget the date: 8/8/88. This was also 43 years and two days after the United States dropped the atomic bomb on Hiroshima, Japan. A group from Japan, visiting Esalen for a conference, invited me to join them for a Hiroshima memorial service that afternoon. They had seen me at the Gazebo Day Care Center, performing for the children in my clown costume. At this time, I still had the word "PEACE" on my clown hat, which had been there ever since the Peace March.

Late in the day, I was sitting in a hot tub, watching the sun about to sink into the Pacific Ocean, the sky a mixture of blazing orange, crimson, and purple. Directly across from me in the hot tub sat a beautiful woman, silhouetted by the sun, her arms extended across the rim of the tub, looking south, her face, and her classic nose, in profile. My first view of Claire. As I looked at her, I felt the kind of synchronicity and magic that I love to be present for. I realized that here before me was the very image that had appeared to me in a dream back in Baltimore in 1970. I woke up so inspired that I stretched a canvas to paint the vision. Claire and I were alone in the hot tub, so I told her about the dream and that I was looking at it, for real, at that moment. We introduced ourselves, and she invited me to join her at her home for a dinner party she was hosting for her friends.

Claire's home, a beautiful creation of her own design, was set atop a location called the Hill of the Hawk, overlooking the Pacific Ocean. The view was breathtaking, a panorama encompassing the ocean, the horizon in the distance, the mountains, and the sky — a spectacular view in all directions.

113

That night, standing outside on her deck, I was in awe of the sky, which was filled with glittering, twinkling stars. I spent a wonderful evening dining, and met and became acquainted with her friends, one of whom was Joseph Campbell. Familiar with Campbell's *Power of Myth* series, I enjoyed this great opportunity to sit in Claire's dining room and listen to Campbell speak about the "Heroes Journey": "The body is the vehicle living the magic of myth. Follow your bliss and don't be afraid; doors will open where you didn't know they were going to be."

This was so true of my own journey, my trusting that the universe would provide what I needed. I would later meet another person I admire and love, Deepak Chopra. I learned from Chopra that:

> Ecology is the metabolic manifestation of information, knowledge and wisdom we experience through genetic evolution. Our mind projects itself out the body through sound, touch, taste, smell and sight. These senses literally shape the texture, the rhythm, and the form of our mind — an amplification of the self-collective homeostatic image we want to be. Each and every cell in our body expresses our intimate relationship with our biological experience, the inner and outer world that makes us one with all.

Sometime later, after leaving her dinner party, I called Claire and explained my predicament, how my van had broken down at the Crossroads and was being repaired. Immediately she invited me to her home again, and even picked me up, taking me back to the Hill of the Hawk.

Claire's home was a unique structure, constructed out of the lumber from an old wooden bridge that she had brought down from the Mendocino area of northern California. The large beams from the bridge's structure were used as the upright and exposed roof support beams. The house was all redwood, with large windows looking out at the spectacular view, standing about 1,500 feet above and overlooking the ocean. Around the ocean-side of the house was a wooden deck. Inside was a large fireplace made from rocks that she had found on the property and brought up from the beach below. The footing rock alone must have weighed a ton. At some point a whale had become beached, and its skeleton had dried under the sun to a bleached white. Taking the skull, Claire had hung it above the fireplace. Everything about the home and its location was special.

Claire's home faced west, affording the most incredible, most magnificent, views of the Pacific Ocean, and of the most amazing, most breathtaking, sunsets and moonsets I have ever seen. Even the fog that crept up from the ocean created magic when it drifted over the land; the gray mist was mystical. When the sun would set between fog and clouds, I just wanted to walk on the clouds in the brilliant orange glow.

When it rained, everything became moist and mystical, the "Myths of Big Sur" so fresh I would just sit there in silence, within a tall grove of redwood trees, listening to the raindrops dripping through the ferns onto the forest floor. When I would look up, a raindrop of pure crystal water falling from the trees would splash on my forehead. The smells of nature would blanket my senses, enveloping me in their comfort, making me feel safe and protected in the loving embrace of Mother Earth.

On the east side of Claire's home was a small swimming pool with a view of the famous Ventana Mountain, sacred to the Esselen Indians. According to an Esselen Indian mythological legend, this mountain was a portal to the other world, through which their ancient ancestors passed into and out of our world. The word *Ventana* means "window" in Spanish. The explorer Portal named the mountain while he was mapping the West Coast.

115

At the top of Ventana Mountain was an open arch of rock that the Esselen Indians called the "Eye to the Universe," which collapsed during the 1906 Earthquake.

It was because the sun and the moon both rise from the east over Ventana Mountain that Claire picked this spot on which to build her home. It was in the center of what she referred to as an electromagnetic grid connected to a Hawaiian heart line, and to Glastonbury and the Chalice Well in England. I later visited the Chalice Well during my 2001 trip to the British Isles, on another quest for love.

Surrounded by the most spectacular views of heaven and nature that I had ever seen or experienced, Claire was the embodiment of her environment. A parapsychologist, Claire's particular clairvoyant gift was the psychokinetic ability to move human emotions. I wanted to become her student, and she became my mentor, the beginning of a relationship and friendship that would change my life in ways I never could have dreamed of. Those who knew her called her a "Whirlwind Dancer"; she could open your mind and heart to horizons beyond your greatest imagination. She had a heart of gold, an intellectual brightness, a loving and compassionate presence.

Claire often held seminars at her home. During the weekend on which Claire and I had met, she hosted Rainbow Hawk, a spiritual Indian guide, who was conducting a three-day Vision Quest on this sacred land. There was a Medicine Wheel, a round circle of rocks with a fire pit in the middle, in an open area north of the house. Its northern direction was aligned with the North Star and the Big Dipper, also known as the Big Bear, constellation; when the Big Bear begins its path across the sky; it serves as an important marker indicating the start of the summer solstice. Months later, I would witness its final winter destination in the sky when I returned in mid-winter.

116

To prepare for the Vision Quest, I camped on a flat area on the cliff that extended out from the land, overlooking the ocean, which afforded a stunning view of the night sky, which was filled with trillions of stars. You could hear the "Coyote Tabernacle Choir" yipping, singing, and serenading throughout the night, adding even more magic to all this splendor. I was fasting, meditating, and earth-walking, breathing deeply, and witnessing poetic glimmers of mystical insights, falling truly in love with the glory and grace of nature's brilliance. Absorbing all this energy produced a thrill that ran through me, resonating to my bones. They call this the "Big Sur Vibration."

A Sweat Lodge had been prepared on the beach for the evening ceremony, the last night of the Vision Quest. The purpose of the Sweat Lodge is to cleanse and purify the body and the spirit, bringing you into harmony in the present with the universal elemental forces so that you can be one with all that is. A fire outside the lodge was heating up the rocks that would be brought into the lodge and placed into the central pit inside. During the ceremony, water would be poured over the rocks, generating steam. The lodge was made of willows, and covered with blankets to block out all outside light. The effect was like being inside a pitch-dark womb.

We entered the Sweat Lodge on our hands and knees, symbolic of being humble to the elemental forces of the universal oneness. We moved clockwise around the central pit. Once everyone was inside and seated around the pit, the heated rocks were brought in and placed in the pit, water was poured over them, and the steam began to rise. The ceremony began, proceeding through four rounds honoring all of the directions: North, east, south, and west, the sun, the moon, the stars, the Earth, and all the Earth's gifts. Rainbow Hawk led the ceremony — drumming, chanting, and singing traditional songs. Everyone shared a concern or their wish for himself or herself, or for someone else, or a vision for world peace.

Upon the conclusion of the ceremony, we exited the Sweat Lodge, proceeding clockwise through the lodge's portal and out onto the beach, where logs had been stuck upright in the sand and set afire. The logs were still burning, the soft ocean breeze scattering glowing embers, looking like fireflies, into the air, lighting a glowing path into the night sky. Shimmering on the water, the moonlight created a radiant glow that lit the way as I walked to the water's edge. Standing there I felt, in that moment, translucent, a feeling of transparency, as I dove into the liquid light. I was returning to the womb of the Earth Mother, bathing my body in her primordial fluids. Under the water, I opened my eyes to see sparkling bioluminescent sea stars glowing. It was like diving into a celestial green fluorescent heaven.

Surfacing, now wrapped in an atmosphere of cosmic stardust, I was surfing across the vast expanse of space itself, feeling like an extraterrestrial being in sympathetic harmony with the essence of the genius of creation. This was truly a blessing, and I am humbly grateful that I was guided here in spirit to receive this sacrament from the Mother of all Creation. A gift acknowledging my presence. Thank you, Claire Chappellet, for your hospitality and for blessing me with your precious presence.

The next day, still charged by the "Big Sur Vibration," we continued the Vision Quest, returning to and lining up before the Medicine Wheel. I was the last in line. Leaving the line, one by one, we approached the wheel from the south. Rainbow Hawk fanned each of us with his eagle feather, directing towards us the smoke of sagebrush burning in an abalone seashell, a ritual we had to undergo before we could enter the Medicine Wheel. Standing perfectly still in the warmth of the sunlight, smelling the sagebrush smoke filling the air, I saw giant cumulus clouds that seemed to take on mystical forms. As my turn came to enter the Medicine Wheel, I suddenly saw, out of the corner of my eye, something coming towards me. I didn't move. As it drew closer, in my peripheral vision, I saw that it was a coyote walking towards me. Everyone in the wheel was watching, gesturing, and pointing, but I didn't want to alarm the coyote. I was standing downwind, and the coyote sensed no danger at my presence. As the coyote passed me, it picked up my scent. The coyote's nose brushed against my leg. Glancing back, the coyote made eye contact with me, and then continued on its way.

The three-day Vision Quest weekend ended with a feast. After the meal we gathered for a sharing circle of our experiences. We all received individual insights about our journeys from Rainbow Hawk before we went our separate ways. Looking me in the eye, he said, "You have been blessed by the coyote's keen sense of survival for your travels." I learned later, in researching Native American folklore, about the mythical character Coyote. I learned that Coyote has a strong sense of survival, and, because of this, is a teacher who points the way through folly and its shortcomings by wit and talent.

I spent another evening at Claire's; the repairs to my van would be completed the next day. Now, with my new friendships, I wanted to stay and discover the Monterey Peninsula area, which includes Big Sur, Carmel, Pebble Beach, Asilomar, Pacific Grove, and Monterey. This would become my new campus in which to develop wisdom and continue being human. It was one of the most inspiring places I have ever been. After picking up my van I began my exploration, discovering a community of artists that came to embrace me like I was family.

Performing was my game, and networking was the method through which I booked my gigs. I would make one appearance, which would lead to others. I found that doing something for publicity was often the best way for me to gain exposure. Getting that contact and a phone number was the key. As I continued performing, I began being called to appear in special events. The pay in these was better; and when my clients

119

liked me, there was a good chance that they would call me back, or even schedule me on their calendars, for future dates.

Tuning into the poetry scene at the cafes, I saw the need for a poetry magazine. So I created just such a publication, *Coyote Bark/Poetic Art*, its title inspired by the Vision Quest at Claire's place. "The Rag," as it was referred to, was a monthly magazine featuring poetry, short stories, and black-and-white art, supported by advertisements. "The Rag" lasted for 11 years.

I had a lot of fun being the publisher and editor of *Coyote Bark/Poetic Art*. "The Rag" led me to some very interesting artists and writers, who provided the material that kept it going for 11 years. To name a few of the contributors: William Giles, Ed Moody, Karen Gelff, John Dotson, Jennifer O'Meara, Janette Hablewitz, Scott Foglesong, Lincoln Tritt, Bonnie Gartshore, Jay Campbell, Ray Magsalay, Alice Jean Small, E. Ashton Winslow, Barbara Bode, Taelen Thomas, Marlie Avanti, Barbara Marx Hubbard, Jessica Ann Davies, Seth Matterson, Laura Burg, Mike Duff, Robert W. Johnston, Davo, Lady Hull, Ruth Richard, Grace Darcy, James Hobbs, Marj Van Peski, Marla O. Piedmont. And these individuals are just the tip of the nose of *Coyote Bark/Poetic Art's* many contributing artists in the Monterey Peninsula area.

I found researching Coyote lore interesting and educational. There is much Native American folklore, and many legends, about the mythical character Coyote. One ancient legend, which seems to be coming true today, is that Coyote had predicted the coming of a "New Age," the time of "Human Greed." And with this New Age would come a struggle to overcome the terrible sorrow of freedom lost. My research led me to formulate the following concept:

> When you hear the coyote's bark, it means that
> you have been invited to become inwardly free,
> to be the master of your own destiny, to take

120

control of your life, to set yourself free, and to walk the path of infinite possibilities, rising to your star-being and beyond.

At two local theater groups, the Grovemont in Monterey and the Forrest in Carmel, I auditioned for parts in *South Pacific* and *Beauty and the Beast*. Getting both parts, I performed through the summer months. The Grovemont Theater kept me working busily for a while, playing parts in a Forest Ranger training program at Fort Ord. In the program they would create different scenarios scripted to put the students through various exercises simulating accidents, disputes, and crimes. This was fun, as we could do anything we wanted within a given story: Take students' weapons or steal their patrol vehicles, hold them hostage, or even escape if we could get away. I also booked myself at the Delmonte, Barnyard, and Crossroads shopping centers. In addition I performed, and taught mime classes, at local schools. This work kept me busy all year round.

During this period, Claire became a very close friend, and I spent a lot of time with her, assisting her with a number of seminars, featuring guest speakers, held in her home.

One day, during a trip down the coast on Highway 1 at Molero, I saw a couple walking along the shoulder of the road. Getting closer, I recognized them to be Ted Turner and Jane Fonda. Ted was sticking his thumb out, trying to hitch a ride. Pulling my van over onto the shoulder, I offered them a ride. They accepted, and Jane got in the back and Ted in the front. Immediately he asked me if I knew who he was. In response, I looked at him and asked if he knew who I was, then told him I was the Peace Clown. Looking in the rearview mirror, I could see that Jane was sitting next to my clown hat, the one with "PEACE" on the brim, the same hat I had worn in 1986 during the Peace March. Ted explained to me that he and Jane were in a hurry to reach their home in Pfeiffer Beach. Larry King was going to interview Ronald Reagan, and Ted and Jane wanted to get to the house in time to catch the interview.

This was actually the second time I had met Jane. The first time was in San Francisco, on Union Street, at the premiere of the movie *Temptation*. On that occasion I had introduced myself and we had spoken briefly. And now, here she was in the backseat of my van, riding with me, a Vietnam veteran. This seemed so ironic. I had often given thought to the possibility of staging some sort of event with Jane, in order to heal the rift between her and the veterans of Vietnam.

Another irony: Here I was, rescuing these two very famous, successful, wealthy people from the side of the road. Jane and Ted: Perfect role models for capitalism, yet both fascinated with leftist revolutionaries. There was even a photo taken of Ted with Fidel Castro, who had rescued Cuba from American capitalism; and one of Jane with Ho Chi Minh, who had rescued South Vietnam from American capitalism. Had I been duped into my role in this picture show? What is my lesson here? Could this be a coincidence, or is my destiny to find out that I am on the wrong side of the wall?

Claire would reserve theater spaces around the Carmel area in order to showcase local talent, as well as talent she attracted from around the world. These events were fund-raising talent shows for Project Planet Earth, a non-profit educational foundation that she had founded. The last such event she put on was in honor of her mother, the most beloved elder in her life. She opened the show by honoring her ancestors; here are a few lines from her eloquent message:

> We are brothers; we are sisters, until every
> person on Planet Earth has freedom. None of us
> truly has it, not materially or spiritually. Let me
> shout loud and clearly with my ancestor Patrick
> Henry, "Give me liberty or give me death."

Liberty to focus on the fulfillment of my destiny, liberty to choose my time to depart. We are free to choose the design and pattern of our lives. Let us choose well; this may be the last chance we have on Planet Earth, our mother, our home sweet home.

The performers were Andrew Wise, flute; Katherine Elber, Tai Chi dancer; Alicia Rete, sounding; Charlie Moore, opening speech; The Rising Stars, gymnastics; Scott Foglesong, slide show; Christy and Alisa Fineman, singing and guitar; and me, mime. Joseph Lyons was the Ringmaster.

Meeting Claire's family was a great opportunity for me. Visiting her parents, Cyril and Patricia Chappellet, at their Pebble Beach home made my relationship with Claire even more special. By the end of 1991 her dad, Cyril, had fallen ill with stomach cancer, and he soon passed away. I drove with Claire a few times when she would stay by her father's side, up until his passing. Her dad's wish was to be cremated and have his ashes sprinkled over Ventana Mountain, the sacred mountain, and his wish was fulfilled on January 10, 1992. Sadly, his were not the only ashes sprinkled over Ventana Mountain that day.

On the winter solstice of 1991, Claire was about to embark on a trip to the East Coast, and held a going-away party at her home. After a beautiful sunset came a magical evening of feasting on a meal created out of edible plants that grew on her land. This was the evening that Claire took me by the hand and invited me to join her on the east deck to view Ventana Mountain and witness the tip of the handle of the Big Dipper, the Big Bear, touching the top of the mountain, the Eye to the Universe, a window to the heavens. That eye, that window, was open now, and I could understand the mythological concept of a portal to the other world.

At that very moment, two shooting stars passed through the Big Dipper, a chilling sight that would only make sense later. Claire squeezed my hand, and we turned to each other and hugged endearingly. She said, "I am leaving now on a trip east. What I want you to do, Hinton, is to stop running from responsibility. You are a very beautiful, creative soul. Focus on your talent." This was the last time I would ever see my precious, dear friend Claire.

CHAPTER TWENTY-EIGHT
MY GUIDING LIGHT, MY GEMINI MOON

Claire asked me to stay at her home through the holidays while she was on the East Coast. During her trip, she visited her friends David and Annie Jubb, who gave training workshops in Whole Brain Functioning Skills for Speed-learning — shifting one's consciousness to increase one's power for effective communications. I had met David at one of the events at Claire's home, and we had connected, hiking together in the Ventana Mountain Range. I found him to be a very gentle, soft-spoken individual, extremely intuitive. We had a wonderful time hanging out together.

During the holidays there were other guests at the house besides me. I had the great fortune to ring in the New Year of 1992 with astrologer Linda Clark. The name may sound familiar; Linda saved two dolphins, a mother and a baby, that had become beached at her home in Redondo Beach, California. Only a day earlier, she had been with Dr. John Lilly, the world's foremost researcher and authority on dolphins, asking him questions about his experiences with dolphins. Linda was later invited to appear on *The Tonight Show* with Johnny Carson, where she recounted her rescue of the dolphins. On the show she observed, "I have learned there are a lot of needs to be met. Too often our good intentions end at our front door, when all we have to do is look outward, as I did that Sunday night."

Linda prepared an astrological chart for my 45th birthday, Saturday, January 4, 1992, a day in which a solar eclipse took place and the sun was in Capricorn; she called it the "Ring of Fire." I celebrated my birthday at Claire's home on the Hill of the Hawk. I should mention that her home was full of wonderful magical treasures, such as a mouse in a red satin dress that pirouetted atop a charm box, and an old stand-up clock that chimed on the hour. Every day was a celebration when Claire was around, and I missed her.

125

My birthday weekend was extremely stormy, and it felt like the house was being shaken to its foundation, like it was going to be blown away by the relentless galling winds and the pounding rain. The electricity went out, and the only light was supplied by a candle and by a fire I lit and kept burning in the fireplace. Despite the bad weather, however, everyone still showed up to celebrate my birthday: Daniel Marracino, Joseph Lyons, Karen Cummings, Joseph Mulholland, J.J. Bear, Jerry Schaffer, and Adam.

The next day, Sunday, January 5, I was all fired up, running around the house with a bear hide over me, beating a drum, chanting, dancing around, full of energy, feeling as though something momentous was about to happen. Stepping outside onto the deck, I stood at the rail and looked out at the ocean. The wind was blowing so hard that I could lean into it, and it would suspend me on air. I called on the elements — earth, wind, fire, and water — integrating them into my being so that I could be one with the forces of nature.

Later, running around the porch out in the yard with Kimo, Claire's white Samoan dog, splashing in the puddles, I had never felt so charged and wild with spirit. Kimo and I ran around until, suddenly, everything grew very quiet, hushed. The rain had stopped, and all you could hear was dripping. Like magic, through pockets in the clouds, light beams and rainbows started appearing all around the property, casting light, like spotlights, on areas at random.

We got word that Highway 1 was clear, and my weekend guests packed and left the house. Lighting a roaring fire in the fireplace, I sat on the bear rug in front of the fireplace, meditating. The telephone rang. I answered it. Jeff Trudeau, a friend of Claire's whom she had been visiting, was on the line. He told me that Claire had died. My heart sank in grief. Tears streamed down my cheeks. Jeff said, "I have my hand on her heart now. We are connected," as I sat in stunned silence,

126

devastated by this sad, terrible news. Jeff described how Claire had taken a bath, put on her white linen dress, lay down in bed, and quietly placed her hands across her chest. With her last words, she said that a celestial angel of light was gesturing, inviting her home. Then Claire took three final breaths and was gone — to Rest in Peace.

A short time later, her mother called to request that I stay at the house while Claire's funeral arrangements were being made. A helicopter would fly the ashes of both Claire and her father, Cyril, to be spread over Ventana Mountain. It was now clear to me why the two shooting stars had passed through the Big Dipper, the Big Bear, on my final evening with Claire, as we stood there together witnessing this magical moment on the winter solstice.

Claire's daughter, Heather, asked me to prepare the Medicine Wheel for a ceremony the evening before the funeral service. Jeff Trudeau was bringing Claire's ashes home from the East Coast. I raked the Medicine Wheel and gathered wood for the fire pit, in silent respect, and placed colored ribbons in all the directions and raised Claire's Earth Flag. Just as the sun was about to set, I lit a fire in honor of the traditions that Claire had preserved here on her property. Keeping the fire burning, I awaited the arrival of Jeff, with Claire's ashes, and the arrival of Carissa, with her grandfather Cyril's ashes. Claire's family members and friends began approaching the Medicine Wheel from the south, and I burned sagebrush and fanned the smoke with Claire's eagle feather to clear each person's energy before they entered the sacred space within the Wheel.

The sunset was one of the most spectacular I have ever seen, as Claire's family and friends gathered together: Her sister, Sybil; her daughter, Heather, and her husband, Sidney; Carissa; Archie; Franklin; Denny; Jeff; David; and me. We stayed there through the night, until the sunrise ushered in the day of Claire and Cyril's funeral service, January 10, 1992. Climbing into the waiting helicopter, Heather held the ashes of Claire and Cyril, and the helicopter lifted off and flew to Ventana Mountain. There, Heather, fulfilling the wishes of her mother, Claire, and her grandfather, Cyril, sprinkled their ashes over the sacred mountain. Now their precious souls could flow into Eternity. Claire and Cyril Chapellet: Two shooting stars passing together through the Eye to the Universe into the other world, to their new home, to their eternal place among the heavenly stars.

My role in Claire's life was now over. As a final, departing tribute, I composed the following poem:

> Thank you for planting the heathers that blossom in the spring, thank you for letting me into your magical world, where we come to play, and watch the sunlight dance, upon the peaceful ocean. I will hold you dear to my heart, Claire. You were my guiding light, a precious gem I will treasure. You have taken your place in the heavenly sky, my Gemini moon. Love and peace, your loving friend, Hinton.

CHAPTER TWENTY-NINE
AN ERA ENDS, A NEW ONE BEGINS

The time had come for me to return to Colorado and the Rocky Mountains, thanks to John Denver once again plucking on my heartstrings. So I set course for Aspen. Selling my van gave me enough money to buy a plane ticket, with a little extra left over to support me until I got settled. I brought *Coyote Bark/Poetic Art* with me, reinventing it after a lesson in marketing placement inspired a change in design. Noticing that it would get lost behind other, larger magazines on bookstore shelves, I made it tall and narrow so that its name could always be seen among the sea of magazines.

An era ended and a new one began, as I settled back in Aspen, a place of some of the most enchanting beauty of nature, protected by a rocky fortress of mountain walls and forests, home to the affluent elite. The mansions standing on the sunny side of the mountains, those with the grandest of views, were filled with every creature comfort imaginable, and sported the richest of interiors. You couldn't help but notice that here lived a different kind of human being, the Elite, far above the common people, high up in the Rockies, above the clouds. I had my own flaws, but I am only human, and now I was predisposed to redefine myself and my conception of a relationship in light of the reality of Aspen's wealthy class. My perception and awareness were being opened to a lavish lifestyle that I never imagined existed.

I was alone again with my journals, my thoughts, my feelings that began to surface, giving expression to deep impulses that I didn't even know I had until putting myself here in Aspen in my $250-a-month room, in an apartment building for low-income people, surrounded by multi-million-dollar homes. Aspen had to have low-income housing for the low-income service workers. No housing, no service workers. Most of the wealthy provided housing for their service workers. Still, the need existed for housing for the labor force employed in Aspen's hotels and restaurants. I was glad to have found my room, which had a shower, a toilet, and a bed, all in one room. Personally, I believe that there should be more housing like this. The majority of people are working all the time these days just to stay in debt. They certainly have no time to be at home, so why have so much space when you are never there to enjoy it?

Settled in, I began my sojourn focusing on my artistic endeavors, wanting to embody the richness this environment had to offer. My challenge was to try and rise above envy, jealously, resentment, and bitterness over my misfortunes.

Anger afflicts so many people. And trying to manage my own anger has always been especially challenging, my parents having been horrible role models — always yelling, always screaming, always being physically violent. Patience is an ally from the insolence that challenges my freedom because I am accessible and learning not to react to attacks, a challenge as well. I admire patience in others, and I want to rise to a greater consciousness within myself. I may not have anything but the ambition to explore new horizons. In any event, this ambition brought me to a place like Aspen. Ultimately, I hope my life will end as gracefully as Great Grandmom's did at 92; she simply passed away quietly, peacefully, in her sleep in her little room in Claremont, Virginia.

Aspen is an intelligent community, with many educational institutions and opportunities: The Aspen Lecture Series at the Gibbons Institute, the Institute of Physics, the Aspen Institute, the Design Conference, the Writers Society, and the Choices for the Future Symposium and the Aspen Center for the Environment. There is also the Film Society's year-round program, the Art Museum, and the Music School with its Music Festival. This time around in Aspen, I resolved to avail myself of these unbelievable educational opportunities.

As "The Rag" had proven to be in the Monterey Peninsula area, *Coyote Bark/Poetic Art* was a great vehicle through which to meet Aspen's artists, to get to know the local business community, and to promote poetry events at the local cafes. One individual I met was Tammy Baar, a clown herself, with a business called Kidtoons. We became close friends, and performed together at many parties and events in the Roaring Fork Valley, including Snowmass's endless Festivals. Many celebrities and businesses held parties that they would repeat year after year, including Mike Douglas, Catherine Zeta-Jones, Don Johnson every fourth of July, the Warner Brothers Ranch, Merv and Thea Addelson, Jon Peters, David Koch, the Aspen Ski Company, and even Saudi Prince Bandar's family. There was plenty to do throughout the year. Even the winter months, skiing season, were filled with parties. Truly, Aspen is a party town.

Continuing my creative relationship with Jon Barnes of the *Ultimate Taxi*, I filmed a few of his special guests, including Jimmy Buffet, Doc Eason, and Steve Skinner. We even took the *Ultimate Taxi* to Las Vegas, documenting the trip and the reactions along the Las Vegas Strip, with local television crews interviewing Jon in the Taxi. It was a lot of fun working with Jon, who has become the most famous taxicab driver in the world and a celebrity in his own right. You could say that he literally did it "His Way."

While in Vegas we checked out the Consumer Electronics Show at the Las Vegas Convention Center. Just outside the Center, something caught my attention. Two artists were writing with chalk on the sidewalk that led to the Center. The artists had written: "Just what the streets of Vegas need, something else that seduces your senses." It was an ad for Zenith, and the artists had also drawn the word "Zenith" with a lighting bolt, the company's logo. I asked them who was behind this, and they told me that it was Massive Media, Inc., an advertising firm out of New York. The technique was very effective, and I noticed similar chalk words and images up and down the main strip on the sidewalk on both sides of the street. What a creative concept, I thought, using chalk art and words stenciled in chalk on the sidewalk as a marketing tool!

CHAPTER THIRTY
GOLF BALL FROM HEAVEN

Back in Aspen, I was walking down the street one day, when a friend came up to me with the sad news that John Denver had died — killed in an airplane crash off Lover's Point in Pacific Grove, California. I had just received a letter from John in which he wrote, "It was a real pleasure meeting you." I had spoken with John earlier in the year, and he said that he had received the story idea I had sent him for a movie in which he would star. In my film, he would portray an astronaut — a solo angel on a star-borne Vision Quest, on a fearless flight far above the Earth, above pain and fear, destined to merge with the celestial stars.

The story involved the flight of a NASA space vessel, *The Constellation Orion*, which embarks on a fact-finding research mission to prove that the Horsehead Nebula in Orion's Belt is an incubator for making stars. After John's death, I revised the story and read it at the candlelight vigil that I organized for him. The vigil was held at the corner of Hyman and Mill, in front of the water fountains created by Nick DeWolf, which bring so much joy to the children in the summer. My revised story went like this:

> John Denver, the Astro-Traveler, is a solo angel on a star-borne Vision Quest, flying on the wings of light, far above the Earth, beyond pain and fear, to be with the celestial angels. He travels through the Milky Way, where each star is the smiling face of an ancient spirit who has blessed us with his or her presence on this place we call Earth. Now cradled in the arms of his Creator, he is embraced in unconditional tender love and compassion. Returning to Orion's Belt, John walks towards a door with a bright star on it. The door opens, and John enters a room,

inside of which sits a large chair, its back facing John, facing a window, smoke rising past a view of the Earth. At that moment the chair turns around and John exclaims, "Oh my God!" as he sees, seated in the chair, George Burns puffing on a cigar. Mr. Burns says, "Welcome home John," and they embrace. John turns, and out of the light appears Jim Henson, who hands John a spark of light. They embrace. John suddenly finds himself on a golf course, and walks along a green fairway. He places the spark of light on a golf tee. He looks to each of the four directions, a John Denver moment, "Sunshine on his shoulder." He swings his magic golf club, sending a gift from heaven in the form of a little white golf ball . . .

. . . found by Bill Twist, on Eldorado Street in Monterey, California.

If you were at John's memorial service at Lover's Point, you heard Bill Twist's story about John losing his golf ball, a Titleist, at Spyglass Golf Course. On the very day that John died, Bill found a golf ball — a Titleist — in the grass by the curb when he arrived at the restaurant on Eldorado Street where he was to meet John for dinner. Sticking the ball in his pocket, Bill entered the restaurant. When John failed to show up, Bill returned to his hotel room, where he learned of John's fatal accident on the news. Bill pulled the golf ball out of his pocket, treasuring John Denver's gift from heaven.

CHAPTER THIRTY-ONE
THE POETS ARE GATHERING

Following the loss of John, I hitched a ride with my friend, Gerry Hosier, to Teaberry, New Jersey, on his private jet. He was very kind about letting me jump aboard when it was just Gerry and his pilot on a flight. Gerry was headed for flight training to obtain his jet certification. From there, it was on to New York City, where I attended The People's Poetry Gathering, sponsored by City Lore and the Poets House, committed to poetry. The language of the heart, the spirit of the word, moving through the population. Words on the sidewalk, words on the Internet. The word is coming out, the poets are gathering.

While in New York City I visited with John and Jean Doswell on their ketch, docked at Pier 63 Maritime on the Hudson River. What a great way to live in New York, spending my first night rocking and rolling as if in the cradle, which is what sleeping on the boat, on the water, reminded me of. The experience, the sensations, brought comfort to my soul.

John Doswell was part of a team of industrious buddies who ambitiously lifted a lighthouse ship from the bottom of Chesapeake Bay, then brought the ship to the Hudson River and restored the vessel. Converting it into a party ship, they named it *Frying Pan*, and docked it at Pier 63 at the end of 23rd Street. On Sunday nights, in the belly of the ship, they had great Jazz.

I went to Peter Beard's Gallery in SoHo to see his *Beauty and the Beast* exhibit, an extreme contrast of images. I had originally met Peter in Aspen during the Aspen Writers Conference and the Summer Words Literary Festival, and we had lunch at the Cantina. I remember how difficult it was to listen to someone talking on about how they had become a writer, what inspired them, where they got their ideas for the material to create a story, etcetera. Madeline Blais was lecturing

135

about how to "Find the Story in Your Experiences," discussing the art of memoirs. How ironic. Here I was having lunch with Peter Beard, the one person who has had the most influence on my memoirs. Peter's journals have inspired my own.

While at the Gallery, I accompanied Peter into the basement, where his painting studio was located. There, we opened our journals and smeared a little paint in them. Dipping a paintbrush into some animal blood, Peter spattered my journal's page for that day with the blood. He always used animal blood in his paintings. He was an animal rights activist, and we shared a love of elephants. After that, we hung out for a while, catching up. He pointed out to me that my journals were too neat, looked too controlled. He told me to loosen up, to be a little freer in putting my journals together. His advice was good, and my journals changed accordingly after that.

Back on the poet's path, in the flow, heading to the poetry event. It sure is fun putting words together; words are the building blocks to knowledge, the path to wisdom, the key to stirring up the imagination. Words bring visions into focus, inspiring creativity, so may our words always inspire others. These were my thoughts as I hung out in front of the Great Hall, Cooper Union, carrying on the tradition of its history of protest, reform, education, and the creative arts. I was writing poetry on the sidewalk with chalk, as people passed and stopped to read the words out loud: "I regard the poet as a sentinel warning us against the approach of the enemies called Bigotry, Lethargy, Intolerance, Ignorance, Inertia, and others members of that brood."

Attending an open mic at the Foundation Building in Room 604, hosted by Ishle Park of the Asian American Writers Workshop, I read from my book of poems, *Why Must Life Rhyme and Reason*. I recited my poem, "No More Pain":

In that last hour when we lose our power and life becomes so plain, because there's no more to gain. You know, when one gets old and the story has been told, just before our death. We are about to take our last breath. Peeking through that portal we thought we were immortal. All alone we are standing when there's no more expanding, finally in that moment the brain stops holding on to all that pain.

After the poetry event I left SoHo. Strolling north on La Guardia Street, I turned and saw the World Trade Center buildings, towering in the sky. Never could I have imagined that this would be the last time I would ever see them. Continuing through Washington Square to the Village, I caught the Metro at the 4th Street Station. As I passed through the tollgate, Dexter Conyers was playing music in the subway, singing "Hard Two Find." After a short underground ride, I popped up at 19th Street.

The Kitchen, located at 512 West 19th Street between 10th and 11th Avenues, was one of my favorite places. Here words were utilized in a variety of very creative ways: Words as visuals, words as performances, words as music, words as dance, words as audience participation. Everything within The Kitchen was covered in words: The floor, the walls, the furniture. Words, words, everywhere.

From there, it was off to a "Midnight Edgar Allen Poe in the Graveyard" event, a group reading of Poe's "The Raven," at the Marble Cemetery. Listening to the poem's verses echoing off stone walls in the dark of night was a unique experience; you had to be there.

Returning late to the dock and the Doswell's ketch, I climbed into bed and drifted off to sleep, in anticipation of more — give me more — words. As I slept, words danced in my dreams, words popped into my mind's eye, words weaved their magic spell, words performed for me.

Surging awake from my poetic dreams, I found my way through another transformational extravaganza of non-stop poetic creativity: Poetry Across Borders. Thank you, City Lore and Poets House, now at Cooper Union, full of the power of the word, the power of poetry, for the people. Onward poetry. What a wonderful treat for myself, feeding my heart and mind with the inspiration of stimulating poetic thinkers, thinkers offering counsel for other poets like me, inspiring me to put pen to paper.

On my way back from The People's Poetry Gathering, I stopped in a town just north of Sioux City, Iowa, on Highway 75, called Hinton. Being in this town was a unique experience because everything had my name, Hinton, on it. The Fire Department, the Post Office, the hardware store, postcards, key chains — all with the name "Hinton." The most fun for me was going to Hinton High School, where the kids sang the school alma mater for me, featuring the lyric, "Hinton we love you." To have a hundred kids singing this touched me. I picked up a couple of t-shirts from the school's Athletic Department, along with anything else for sale in town that had "Hinton" on it.

I stopped in Denver, where my friend, Bud Wilson, told me about the National Youth Leadership Conference at the Hilton in the Plaza Ballroom. One of the speakers at the conference was Jonathan Kozol, a teacher, activist, and author, whose most recent book at the time was *Ordinary Resurrections*. Kozol has been referred to by conservatives as a liberal with good intentions, and has been accused of writing about things that only he knows about. His response is, "I have eyes, I can see."

Early in his teaching career, Kozol was fired from Boston Public School for presenting poetry to his students and assigning the works of Langston Hughes. At the conference he pointed out that the only mistake a person can make is waiting too long to take action. He said, "Young people are not the future, they are the present," encouraging everyone "to think long term because it is a commitment to making a difference in the world." He also said, "Take risks, you will survive, it can lead to new opportunities." He quoted Chavez: "Some give time, some give their lives."

He said that in our society, unfortunately, children have price tags on their foreheads when they walk into a classroom, based upon the social position or color of them and their families. But every child is special and should be approached as a small, precious gift to be opened with gentle, loving care. I truly wish that my parents had learned and practiced this philosophy at some time during their lives.

From Denver I headed back to Aspen. Every year since my arrival there, I had attended the Design Conference. At the most recent conference, I had reflected upon the idea that "The more things change, the more they stay the same." Bran Ferren, Co-chairman and Chief Creative Officer for Applied Minds, Inc., and a senior advisor to several agencies on advanced technology, put it very simply: "[Technology] is out of control and if you were afraid of technology before, well the age of anxiety is going to kill you, or it can be serious fun." We are only just beginning on the path towards the ultimate potential of technological innovation, and today it is our intuitive mind that technology seems to be modeling. It was also brought to my attention that there are two types of people, each type seeing things differently: Dyslexic people, who see everything all at once, and ordinary people, who focus in on detail more easily. Being dyslexic myself, I was inspired to express, in words, the influence that the conference had on me: "I am a design with a purpose; my intention is to design."

Aspen is known for its eccentric characters. Among the more famous was No Problem Joe, who, whenever he got arrested for drunk and disorderly conduct and thrown in jail for the night, would always say, "No problem." Aspen named a bridge downtown after him. There was Ralph Jackson, the Prince Ski Bum, a bust of whose head stands on Ute Avenue. There was Hunter Thomas, the notorious gonzo writer who ran for Sheriff and wrote for *Rolling Stone Magazine*, who hung out at the Woody Creek Tavern. Perhaps Thompson's most famous novel, *Fear and Loathing in Las Vegas*, was made into a movie starring Johnny Depp. There is Bob Braudis, the Sheriff of Aspen for many years, with his big gap-toothed smile, who is also world-famous himself. And there is Mary Hayes, who writes a gossip column for the *Aspen Times* newspaper. All of them unique Aspen characters.

Speaking of newspapers, there was a steady flow of letters to the editor, from none other than yours truly, about my poetry trips, such as one I took to New Mexico. I called this trip the "New Santa Fe Way, the Crossroads of Cultural Rebellion." The trip was a rendezvous at a point in time that proved beneficial for all present at the Aztec Café, a chance to meet as if in free nature. It offered more than just wild behavior; the slam-yourself poets screamed words from the podiums of personal confessions, where the illegal substance was poetry dope. Having no fear of entangled emotions, looming indeed and provoking insights. Lost were old ways of expressing truths. There were long-haired, short-haired, pierced, tattooed bodies sporting styles and fashions from no discernible time period. The world's greatest rebels at an androgynous tribal free-for-all. Along the Santa Fe Way, fires were lit, new words created and traded over steaming coffee brews in cafes, where once had stood sun-dried prairies, the gathering places of ancient ones adorned in buffalo robes, painfully bargaining away old nomadic ways.

CHAPTER THIRTY-TWO
THE MAGICAL POETRY BUS

On a trip to Chicago, I visited Cathleen Schandelmeier, a raw, energetic spirited poet, "Cat" is who I call her, reminds me of a jaguar saw the light of social change and the importance of communications. She said to me, "There's a raging frustrated heart-broken generation feeling oppressed wanting to speak its mind. The poor, and I don't mean money — the emotionally neglected and unheard — have had enough and aren't going to take it anymore." Handing me her book of poems entitled, *Suck My Toes and I'll Follow You Anywhere"*, she reminded me that, "The only rich poets are dead poets. After thirty-two years of writing, the postage is still a bigger expense than the revenue earned."

While sitting at Cat's kitchen table, I heard Buffalo Springfield on the radio ("Stop, look, what's that sound . . ."), making me think of the emancipation of individuals crying out for freedom of expression. This unharnessed energy, burgeoning, about to explode, possessing enormous potential. Cat's husband, Pete Bartel, a jazz trumpet player, spoke his wisdom: "I don't think of giving up my identity or freedom. I see it as digestion, merely a transformation on a superficial level. I'm not being devoured like a bowl of Cheerios. Instead, I'm becoming a part of something larger."

In September 1997, Cat planned a trip, "The Magical Poetry Bus Tour," to New York City and Central Park's Bandshell for Allen Ginsberg's memorial. There, 85 poets from around the world would try to fit "100 pounds of words into a 50-pound bag," each poet allotted two minutes at the microphone. Behind the wheel of the bus, Cat drove like she read poetry — with aggressive confidence. She told us the story about the tattoo on the back of her head — the Egyptian Eye, the Left Eye of Horus, also known as the Night Eye. Cat's Eye. At one point, driving at night, we found ourselves passing through

141

pouring-down rain so heavy that we couldn't see 10 feet in front of the bus. Cat's Eye, the same eye that saw Osiris back from the dead, guided us safely through the downpour, sparing us from becoming "The Dead Poets Society." The Left Eye of Horus is a symbol that means "to think, to do, to be, to act." It is, in essence, an action verb.

We arrived, under rainy skies, at the Central Park Bandshell. The Patriots of Poetry were now present, having traveled from distant places to gather and share the feelings expressed in their faces, in their eyes, in their words, revealing their true nature, discovering the truth that "We are One." Whenever I mentioned that I was from Aspen, the first thing everyone asked me was, "Do you know Hunter Thompson?" Poets at the Ginsberg memorial included Patrick Fenton, reading from *Kerouac in Queens*; Brigid Muraghan, from her poem about Ginsberg's *Howl*; and Mary Rudge, from her book, *She Can't Be Beat*. And here, in Central Park, "The beat goes on," even in the rain.

After the memorial, Cat, Pete, and I treated ourselves to the masterpieces of our favorite Postimpressionist artists, at the MOMA, the Museum of Modern Art, at 11 West 53rd Street: Marc Chagall's "The I and the Village," Pablo Picasso's "Two Acrobats with a Dog," Henri Rousseau's "The Sleeping Gypsy," and, perhaps my favorite, Vincent van Gogh's "The Starry Night."

Toot! Toot! The little Magical Poetry Bus chugged out of New York City, the lyrics of a Beatles song coming over the radio: "Baby you can drive my car, yes I'm gonna be a star . . . Beep beep'm beep beep Yeah!" Suddenly a scream of jubilation from Cat; the sun was finally coming out! The roadside flowers were beautiful, everything shining, as we headed back to Chicago. Pete launched into the song, "Sunshine on my Shoulder," which always makes me think of John Denver.

142

Looking up from a new story she was working on, Cat said, "Hinton, everyone is birthed by a sacred star, your word 'Intelligenes' has got me inspired. It's time to celebrate our genius and you are a character in my story, you are the wizard named Peace Earth Walker. Pete is the noble knight Samuel Clamor, and I am the Princess Emerald Mountain Whoop, and we are on a quest for the Secret Mantra." Three curious travelers on an adventure in their Magical Poetry Bus, traversing the highways and byways, dispensing the genius of the word among the masses.

We stopped in Kent, Ohio, and the Crosby, Stills, Nash, and Young song, "Four Dead in Ohio," came to mind, in honor of the date, May 4, 1970. The date on which those four shots rang out, reverberating across the "Land of the Free," taking the lives of Alison Krause, Jeffrey Miller, Sandra Scheuer, and William Schroeder at Kent State. We were in town to share our poetry at an evening reading at Cat's Impetuous Books and Stuff Store. Cheryl Townsend, also nicknamed "Cat," greeted us at the door. The Patriots of Poetry had arrived at this stop along their quest; let the Secret Mantra be heard.

After the reading, we returned to Chicago. As we traversed the Sky Way to the North Beach Poetry Gathering, the radio was playing, "There is something in the air." Nothing could have been more appropriate. At the Gathering, next to Muscle Beach, due east of the Chess Pavilion, under a willowy willow tree, poets in the Windy City gathered, taking their rapport very seriously, not just barking in the wind. I felt like I was experiencing something special here in the City of Champions. Chicago, a town of monuments to architectural wonder: I dedicate this to Ignacio Carrea-Ortiz, my architect friend, who lived in Chicago at that time.

The day after the Gathering, I just had to go and experience Wrigley Field and watch a Chicago Cubs game before leaving the city. That day the Cubs were playing the third

143

game in a best-of-three series against the San Francisco Giants. Down two games, the Cubs rallied and won. That evening, my last in Chicago, we cruised to the Green Dolphin Street Jazz Club, where the sound of the Dolphin Spirit penetrated so deeply into my consciousness that, for a moment, I thought I actually saw dolphins on stage playing music. Cat's husband Pete took center stage and wailed on his trumpet, with Jose Valdez on piano with his combo of musicians. Sitting at the bar, sipping a Guinness, I howled and whooped it up. Chicago. My kind of town.

On the way back to Aspen, I stopped in Boulder, where the Beat Book Shop, on Pearl Street, owned by Tom Peters, had put together an evening poetry reading. That night the moon was full and the sidewalk cafe at Penny Lane was buzzing. You could feel the magic as you entered the coffee shop house, referred to as "The gathering place for locals." Everyone had gathered with a fine-tuned "third ear." Mingling, I approached Tom, who asked me, "You want to take the open mic?" And with that I was on stage, stepping into the spotlight. Adjusting the mic, I centered myself and glanced around the room. I had everyone's attention:

> "Always treat language like a dangerous toy." Those are the words of Anselm Hollo. Let's look at the word "FUCK"! This word is so much a part of our daily language. There are so many things we have become accustomed to. If words are dangerous then there's nothing more irritating than phrases in discourse that are constantly in our minds like someone with a weapon holding us hostage: "I am fucked!" It is as though we are emotionally paralyzed. Because it is all about communicating a single idea, a few "fucks and grunts." It seems prehistoric. We are afraid of everything and each other and the world is a beautiful place but we make it an ugly place where ignorance and

144

prejudice lead to intolerance and conflict. The American Dream is the big disappointment. What will happen to those who will not be the beneficiaries of a fulfilled enriched life of liberty and the pursuit of material happiness?

Following my return to Aspen, I left again, driving a friend's car to San Antonio, Texas, with a poetry stop in Austin. Driving off Highway 35 South, and exiting on Sixth Street downtown, I reached my first red light. While I was stopped, a man in a pink bikini and thigh-high high-heeled patent leather boots crossed in front of me in the pedestrian crosswalk. He was carrying a sign indicating that he was running for mayor. My first impression of Austin. *This must be a far-out town*, I thought.

Looking for some poetry action, I arrived at the Art Plex at Seventeenth and Guadalupe. Soon I was hanging out on the rooftop in a poetry gathering, a Wells Fargo sign overlooking the assemblage of people. A few electronic adjustments — and then we were treated to the sounds of an artistic instrumental improv jam. The poets having assembled, the flow of creativity erupted. To be present, to "Be Here Now," on the rooftop, is what it was all about. This event had been inspired by Harold McMillan, the heart and soul of the event.

Harold was also the organizer of the Austin Jazz Festival, where I found myself on the same stage that had just been graced by Stefo Harris, one of the most accomplished, innovative, and creative jazz vibraphonists in the world. The mic was open, the spotlight wanted a voice to be heard, and I was up:

Texas, this vast land that has become ethnically rich with spirits drawn here of independent nature. To grandeur reflected in all its natural beauty, a collection of folksy treasure in a friendly climate. With an easygoing sense of humor in a confident way. Where big night skies

145

reflect the twinkle in their eyes, a loving openness that spreads like the breathtaking beauty across the prairies and plains. From horizon to horizon, rainbows that seem to float in the sky over golden buffalo grass between rolling hills, sandy beaches, tropical valleys, and fields of flowers, desert, and sage. So y'all breathe deep the legends and myths romanticized by lightning-inspired images from yuppie to gypsy poets of a new Ameritexatonian in the Lone Star State. Aspiring to be free, only serving the higher self, deep in the heart of a true Texan is the famous motto, "I am besieged. I shall never surrender or retreat," from a poet's heart for independence.

CHAPTER THIRTY-THREE
SWEET, LITTLE, PRECIOUS SOULS

Back in Aspen my good friend, Bud Wilson, called to tell me that he was working with an organization called Earth Walk, Nature Centered Life Learning Institute on an adventure in Moab, Utah. He wanted to know if I would join him, as a volunteer counselor for a two week experience, including a River Rafting Trip down the Colorado River, with nine Vietnamese and Cambodian refugee children, I accepted without hesitation. This adventure would turn out to be my most rewarding and healing experience since my return from Vietnam. It was so pleasant, so comforting, being with those nine children, those sweet, little, precious souls. Together we explored the wonders of nature, and the friendships I made on this adventure reminded me of moments I will carry in my heart forever from Vietnam. In Vietnam, it had always been the children who kept me in the present. Children, always the most innocent victims of the madness of war.

As we rafted down the Colorado River, my favorite moments were the impressions the children made on me as individuals: Listening to their laughter, to their jokes, to their teasing; how they loved to tease. Looking into their precious little faces and the reflections in their eyes, what did I see? Myself and the pure love of innocents. I felt joy in learning their names and sharing all the moments we spent together through the days and nights. I cherished seeing their individual uniquenesses, their strengths, their weaknesses, their fears. Not having any children of my own, the parental experiences I gained on this adventure were very fulfilling and grounding. Patience and being present for their needs was more important than anything else that I had to do or wanted to do.

My love for all people on this precious place we call Planet Earth was reinforced by these children. Their fascination with me brought back, and brings back today, the good memories I always had of the children of Vietnam. My complexion and red hair were curiosities to them, and I loved the attention they gave me. It is always the children who keep me in the present. If I could scoop up into my arms all the children in the world, those innocent victims of the madness of war, I would take them to a place beyond right and wrong, to a place of love and peace beyond the reach of the monsters who wage war.

The realization, for me, is that we are the acts of our compassion; only I can take responsibility for my behavior. Being kind, acting out of the heart, my mind letting the nature of my loving heart shine, guiding me to do what I am here to do, being free, flowing in the present — that is what it was like to be with those children. They were each a gift, and as I looked around at them, I felt blessed to be in their presence.

Our duty is to be people of integrity, to be loving and compassionate and faithful — taking responsibility for our actions, being thoughtful, respecting ourselves and the dignity of others around us. At all times we must be aware and alert, our hearts in agreement with the vision of the Earth Peace Walkers.

And so, to director Bud Wilson, to assistant Susan Swern, to volunteer counselor Jude Lucero Witashek, and to the nine little precious star-beings — Shirley Dang, Tony Le, Dang Nguyen, Hoang Nguyen, Tony Pham, Jun Phan, Tai Vu, Christian Lewis, and Jeremy Pedrin: Thank you all for blessing me with your presence.

148

CHAPTER THIRTY-FOUR
WHISPERS OF FORGIVENESS

September 12, 1999. I received a phone call that my Dad, Hinton Edward Harrison, Sr., had passed away. Calling my friend, Gerry Hosier, I shared the news with him. Gerry told me that he was going to Washington, DC, and he invited me to accompany him that far on his private jet, which was close enough to Baltimore for me. Arriving in DC, I caught a bus to Baltimore.

Dad's service was held at the Methodist Church, located at the corner of 4th Street and Pontiac Avenue, just half a block from Dad and Rose's row house. Born just two doors down from the house, on the same street, Rose had spent her entire life in the neighborhood.

During Dad's service, friends shared their condolences, memories, and stories; and I shared a poem entitled, *Whispers of Forgiveness*.

And now, in the pages of this book, I would like to offer to Dad this message:

> Life is a great mystery in every moment, then death comes and we cannot comprehend. Fate is wordless, and destiny is not written. Love is no guarantee. The future we will not know, and shadows fall upon the strongest of hearts. My face is pressed in the palms of my hand. I weep, and my answer is the echo of my crying. I feel nothing but the wetness of my tears. But then love comes and wipes my tears away, for love is everything and gives us the wisdom we need. From the lips of the dead come no words. But if I listen, in the distance shines a star that sounds of love, unlocking from deep in my heart the

best of memories. Dad, your lifestyle was simple and humble, and you had your ups downs. But, Dad, I will always be grateful for the gift of life you gave me. I appreciated the good times and things, like our favorite fishing spots and the walks in the forest, the silence in its sanctuary broken only by the wind blowing through the pine needles. Those are the special moments I will treasure as I try to forget the bad times. You have been set free from a convalescent prison, set free from your aging and decaying body, to live a fuller life cradled by your Creator. For it is not darkness we go to, but to the beautiful company of light, peace, and eternal love. In the end, success and failure are the same; the only real democracy is death itself. Your soul is free now. No more pain. Hear my whispers of forgiveness. God Bless You, and May You Rest in Peace.

Eight years later, on May 17, 2007, my stepmother, Rose Elizabeth Padgett-Harrison, passed away at the age of 77. During Rose's final illness and up until her death, her niece, Patsy Padgett-Krasowski, cared for her. This was the same Patsy, my older cousin, who had helped find me after I ran away from home at 14.

As an adult, whenever I had been in Rose's presence, I felt emotionally crippled with anger and rage, as the painful memories of the horrific abuse I suffered at her hands came flooding back into my mind, overwhelming me. My heart would pound and race, my blood would feel like it was boiling. I would become agitated, irritable, and hostile. I would aggressively confront her verbally about the abuse. *I begged you, Step Mommie Dearest, please hurt me no more!*

As a man of peace, finding myself possessed by such an ugly emotional state, an emotional tyranny if you will, was frustrating. It made me feel strange, as though I was in the grip of some hellish chemical imbalance. In short, that heart-pounding blood-boiling state of anger and rage was NOT me, was not the way I wanted to be. Whenever I found myself in this state, it was clear to me that I needed help in dealing with anxiety and depression — before they killed me.

But that was then and this is now, and Rose is in the world no longer. And so, in peace and with no anger or rage, I would like to offer this message to Rose: May you Rest in Peace; and may the prickly thorns cause no more tears of blood.

And to Patsy I would like to say, God Bless You for being there and caring for Rose.

CHAPTER THIRTY-FIVE
JUST ENOUGH

Following Dad's service, I spent a few days in Baltimore, then returned to Aspen, where I still had an apartment. Once in town, I headed to the Rio Grand, a hiking and biking trail running along the Roaring Fork River. I pondered what my life would be like now that Dad was gone. What would be my motivation now? Walking along the Rio Grand, breathing in the beauty of the moment, I suddenly came upon a small round object on the ground before me. What was this object that was lying here waiting to be discovered? It was a miniature ball of earth. Gracefully and gently cupping this precious gift in my hands, I bowed my head humbly, pausing a moment for an insight, then I raised my hands to the sky. *Great Spirit, is this a message for me?* I silently asked. Attaching my newfound treasure to a piece of string, I fashioned a necklace and hung it around my neck, listening with all my heart for what this omen could possibly mean.

Continuing down the trail, I met Stephan Shearer — outdoor adventurer, an amazing man, older than me, in great shape who could out-hike a mountain goat. He asked, "How would you like to go to Utah?" It was synchronicity, as I was ready for another adventure. So again began an odyssey, a lesson in brotherly love and friendship on the road, an opportunity to view the great marvels of nature, to just listen to nature.

Colorado National Monument, one of America's boldest, biggest, and most brilliantly colored plateau-and-canyon landscapes, was right here in our very own backyard. As the day drew to a close, the view of the sunset was breathtaking, spectacular. On the first night, we camped on the rim rock of the Grand Valley of the Colorado River outside Grand Junction.

The next morning, aboard "Just Enough," the Volkswagen bus serving as our transportation, we drove into

Utah on I-70, making a left turn at Cisco onto Highway 128 and heading for Moab. As we proceeded, we could see the beautiful white and red sandstone walls along the Colorado River. Reaching the location where the Dolores and Colorado Rivers join together at the Dewey Bridge, we set up camp. That night, we camped under a full moon that climbed the softly rounded peaks, which resembled flesh-like breasts, the moonlight making them glow. Sitting there, we gazed at the stars. In the distance, the calls of wild turkeys echoed in the canyon.

The next morning we arose early, just as the sun began to rise, to hike the rims of the vertical cliffs overlooking the confluence of the two rivers — a vista of cottonwoods along fertile valleys ripe with grass and flowers in bloom. After roaming for a while, we headed back to camp, where Stephan prepared cornmeal mush with peanut butter and honey. I ate nothing, however, because, at the beginning of this trip, I had begun a fast, aided by the Master Cleanser: Lemon juice, maple syrup, and cayenne pepper. To me, this journey was more than just a mere road trip, and I felt compelled to listen to and process my feelings.

Breaking camp, we continued towards Moab, stopping along Highway 128, just before reaching Highway 163 into Moab. At that location are springs, from which we collected some water. This water is so sweet that the springs are called Matrimony Springs; drink from them, and you feel so good that you just might go out and get married! Proceeding on, we hung a right turn onto 163 and headed up to the Klondike Bluffs, where we set up camp on the ground under an overhang that looked out towards the La Sal Mountain Range. As Stephan heated up some water for soup, we thought about where to go next: Capitol Reef or Lake Powell? Deciding to defer our decision, we climbed into our sleeping bags and bedded down for the night.

The next morning, as soon as the sun peeked over the La Sal Mountain Range, we quickly crawled out of our sleeping bags, and climbed onto the overhang to watch the sunrise. I performed my morning sun salutation, honoring all the directions: Deep peace to the running waves, deep peace to the flowing air, deep peace to the quiet Earth, deep peace to the shining stars, deep peace to the sons and daughters of peace, deep peace to all creation. Thank you, Great Spirit.

We decided to head west towards Boulder, Utah, so it was back onto I-70, west to 24, south to Hanksville, west on 24 to Torrey, and south on 12 down towards Boulder. Reaching Boulder, we embarked on a journey down the Burr Trail. We traversed switchbacks down through Studhorse Peaks, and continued on to the Notom-Bullfrog Road in the Water Pocket Fold, where the multi-layered rock of the plateaus, mesas, and buttes suddenly stands on edge, like gigantic dominoes caught in mid-fall. Truly an amazing gift that Mother Earth has given us, the many layers of her being. Then it was up onto the mesa above Grand Gulch for a spectacular drive across another world. We finally ended up at Bullfrog Basin, looking across Lake Powell; waiting to board the John Atlantic Burr Ferry to Hall's Crossing.

At Hall's Campground my close friends, camp hosts Stanley and Dorothy Swim, prepared a dinner of freshly caught stripers that looked and smelled divine — all the more so as I was still fasting. After a blessed hot shower and a deep sleep, Stephan and I awakened to waves of magenta clouds streaming in from the eastern horizon to the Henry Mountains. Referred to locally as "the Little Rockies," the Henry Mountains were formed by igneous extrusions, called "laccoliths," that formed domes in the rock above them but never broke through — volcanoes that didn't erupt.

Presently, we were on the road again in "Just Enough," continuing on this odyssey that we hoped would never end. Proceeding down Highway 276, we reached Highway 261 South — the "Trail of the Ancients." At the Switchback Overlook we

155

stopped to stretch and take in the view. Then we journeyed on through the Valley of the Gods to Mexican Hat, and took Highway 163 down into Monument Valley through the Navajo Reservation, stopping by the road to check out the Navajo artists in their wooden lean-tos. West at Kayenta onto Highway 160, then up Highway 98 to Page, where we replenished our supplies and washed our laundry — which, in my case, was just the clothes I was wearing, which were "just enough."

Continuing on, we crossed the Glen Canyon Dam as quickly as we could. With all of the strange headlines in the news about extremist bombings, and knowing that many people wanted this dam to be gone, we drove on, anxious to get off the damned dam. Reaching Big Water and Warm Creek Bay, we stopped for a wake-up dip in the lake. Then it was on to Smoky Mountain Road, a feat of human engineering, which proved to be the challenge of a lifetime for "Just Enough." In the past, this stretch of road had been recommended for 4-wheel-drive vehicles. However, the road had been recently graded, which was just enough to make it possible for "Just Enough" to negotiate it.

Some people said we couldn't make it. They even told us that there was nothing out there but sagebrush, gray clay, and rattlesnakes. Why in the world would anyone want to go up there in the first place? (Unless they were up to something useful like mining coal or uranium.) But we took on the challenge in a spirit of confidence and faith, in order to experience another wonder, the Grand Staircase-Escalante National Monument (Thanks, Uncle Bill). Driving on until dusk, we stopped and set up camp on the Kaiparowits Plateau, a high, wide, open space on which the horizon extended in all directions as far as the eye could see.

From sunset to sunrise Stephan and I were treated to a cosmic view of countless stars in the round planetarium dome of de-light in the night sky, the heavenly show accompanied by the Kaiparowits Coyote Tabernacle Choir. Looking deep into the embers of our campfire, watching the last flames dance out into the night, I was filled with the immensity of life on this plateau. So many different life forms, all existing in such a delicate balance. All I needed to do was open my eyes and look closely, for nature reveals itself to those who sit still. I was truly grateful to Stephan, my brother and friend, as I sat by the fire under the stars.

It was long into the night before I could go to sleep. The moonlight was shining in my face as a soft breeze of ancient beings whispered through the oasis of twisted junipers, pinions, and pines that surrounded our campsite. As I closed my eyes and drifted off to sleep, I wished that this night could last forever.

I awoke to the birds singing their sweet melodies and the warmth of the morning sun shining on my face. As I rose to look at the horizon, the 360-degree spectacle all around me, I was spellbound by what a blessing all of this grandeur was. After honoring all that I saw, we broke camp, boarded "Just Enough," and, with feelings of regret at leaving this beautiful spot, took off down the road towards our next destination, Escalante, a small, quiet town in an oasis valley.

Along the way, we stopped at a local market for some fresh vegetables for Stephan; although 10 days into our trip, I was still fasting. We proceeded on Highway 12, the "Scenic Byway," towards Boulder, traveling along a beautiful rock-spine ridge to the Old Boulder Mail Trail — a "cross country" route down canyon walls and up slick rock saddles once used by the Mormons to deliver mail between Escalante and Boulder.

Just before reaching Boulder, we stopped and hiked through an area featuring a back-country landing strip with an old airplane mounted nose-down in the ground, serving as a "tower," with the words "UFO Landing Strip" brushed onto its belly and a windsock attached to its tail. The terrain varied from sand mesas to rock cliff canyons, looking like a miniature

Yosemite. A physically demanding hiking experience, the 16-mile trail back to Escalante affords hikers many days of exploring the mesas and side canyons. Unfortunately, we were coming to the end of our odyssey.

On the road once more, we took Highway 12 to Torrey, then Highway 24 back to I-70. Heading east towards Colorado, we approached Thompson just as it was getting dark. Stephan suggested that we camp for the night in Thompson Canyon, and check out some impressive petroglyphs in the morning. These particular rock art paintings, dating from 7000 B.C., suggest that this location could have been a holy place where ancient people followed a simple, social lifestyle, and gathered together to share their experiences. More than enough to keep me humble about my own lessons learned in living simply on the Earth, I pondered, as we motored back to Aspen in "Just Enough."

CHAPTER THIRTY-SIX
FASTING COYOTE

Back in Aspen after my adventure with Stephan, I was working on a poem in a copy store one day, creating one of my greetings cards with a picture and poem on it, when my cell phone rang. It was my friend, Connie Marlow, wanting to know if I would drive with her to Glendale, California, to do some work on the house that she owned there. Having nothing pressing going on at the moment, I said, "Sure, let's go." And soon we were off down the highway.

Arriving in Glendale early the next morning, we stopped at her house and rested for the day, and then had dinner. That evening, Connie received a phone call from a friend, who had a show called *Awareness*, inviting Connie to her house that night to meet a shaman, named Kuichy, from Cusco, Peru. While on the phone, Connie turned and asked if I wanted to go hear Kuichy speak as well. I readily accepted the invitation, as this was too cool an opportunity to pass up.

Actually, this opportunity was fortuitous as well. In 1995, Connie had started a project called "Peace and Healing in the Americas," which involved our traveling through Mexico for three months. On March 21st, 1995, the spring equinox, we were present at Chichen Itza for the descent of the astronomical alignment of the Serpent of Light.

This trip was very special because, while visiting the ancient ruins in the northeast state of Chiapas, the temple most interesting to me was the Mayan Palace at Palenque, an observatory built to study the stars. The Maya believed that they came from the stars, and were called the Children of the Stars, who came here pre-encoded with the mission to create their dream. They knew who they were before coming into the physical world, something that resonated within me, a child of the stars not attached to the material world but just visiting this planet and experiencing the gift of life, a manifestation of starlight within. The term Tree of Life comes from the Maya, who could connect with the supernatural. During my visit, I had the great opportunity to hang with Moises Morales, one of the archaeologists of Palenque, who shared the story of the famous sarcophagus of the Tomb of Pakal, which featured an illustration of an astral traveler.

On this trip to Mexico, I went on a quest for coyote mythology as part of my research in creating *Coyote Bark/Poetic Art* magazine, "The Rag." Just outside of Mexico City, I discovered *Nezahualcoyotl*, a town named after the Aztec Poet King Nezahualcoyotl, who was born on April 28, 1402, the Day of the Rabbit in the Year of the Deer, according to the Aztec calendar. As a child he learned, through great suffering and hardship, the reality and value of life. When the boy was 12, a powerful Toltec army invaded his father's kingdom. When the situation became hopeless, his father fled with him into the jungle. Hiding him in a tree as the enemy approached, his father said, "My dearly loved son, lion's arm, I am forced to depart from this life." And, from his hiding place among the branches of the tree, he watched helplessly as the warriors murdered his father.

In that moment, he was transformed from prince to jungle boy, and embarked upon a series of wanderings, exploits, and hair-raising escapes that led his contemporaries to believe him to be a divinely aided master of magic and trickery. The boy was very coyote-like, and eventually found sanctuary with his kinsmen. In time he became a master diplomat who, in 1431, regained the crown of his father's stolen kingdom. As king, he led his people into an era of advanced civilization that was the equal of the Greeks' Golden Age, and established a university where sages fostered a cultural renaissance that brought the Aztec traditions to their highest level of expression.

His name became *Nezahualcoyotl*, meaning "Fasting Coyote," implying self-control and humility towards life. The Omnipresent Spirit, the Lord of Everywhere, was the guiding light of his philosophy. There was no image to represent this deity, whose home could not be fixed. "God, our Lord, is invoked everywhere. Everywhere is He venerated. It is He who creates things. He creates Himself, God."

Nezahualcoyotl disapproved of mass sacrifices, and dreamed of ending the cults of his time. He pondered the legend of Quetzalcoatl, the Priest King and reformer, who was driven away from his center and empire of intellect. Nezahualcoyotl spent his life mastering poetry, philosophy, and supporting music and dance. He honored the heroes of art, those that valued life. He was the poet of the love of life and the most prolific writer of his time, writing 36 volumes containing his philosophy and describing his investigations into nature, the functions of poetry, songs, flowers, and meditations on the relationship of man and Divinity. He had great compassion for the poor, the sick, the widowed, and the aged; and he spent much of his wealth in feeding and clothing the needy, especially during famine years.

Nezahualcoyotl was also a great designer, his architecture creating a small universe around him that reflected his love for the abundance of life. He enjoyed a palace, a menagerie, and fantastic gardens that were famous in his time; and he created the center of learning and philosophy where he could come to rest and contemplate the other world. As he walked the paths through his treasured floral gardens on the highland overlooking his kingdom, he pondered his life. Because of this belief in the Omnipresent Spirit, he felt a sense of peace and harmony with all things. He gave no validity to depressive thoughts, for there was no time for such worry in life, which was so precious and short. Nezahualcoyotl wrote:

161

We are not here for always/But only tarry for a short while/Though it be of gold it will break/Though it be a quetzal feather it will come apart/Nothing lasts for ever on earth/But is only here a little.

We all fade away and are consumed by time, he knew. He believed that the Earth is a borrowed home, is temporary, and is not the home of man, and that we have to abandon it soon. Therefore, he lived a life of free association, and believed poetry was a gift loaned to us to make easier our path through this life that should be a celebration.

Nezahualcoyotl loved flowers, and felt that they bring us into the moment and inspire poems that allow us to get to know ourselves. We express and get in touch with our feelings and humanity, and so return to Divinity — that place of the intangible and bodiless. He believed that happy are those who can enjoy the flowers, for truly they are the happiest beings and the way to the great mystery of existence, to the knowledge of transcendence.

The Poet King Nezahualcoyotl — "Fasting Coyote" — the poet of the love of life, the teacher of self-control and humility towards life. Leader of a great civilization just 50 years before the arrival of Cortez in 1519.

More than 500 years later, on Connie's and my journey for "Peace and Healing in the Americas," Machu Picchu, in Peru, was to have been one of our stops as well, but we never made it. However, Machu Picchu was still calling me, and I couldn't stop thinking about it. And soon, I would answer its call.

CHAPTER THIRTY-SEVEN
THE SNOW STAR

Entering the house of Connie's friend, my attention was immediately drawn to a man sitting on the couch. He was dressed all in white, holding a Condor feather in his hand, his hair extending down to his waist — a sweet, glowing person full of light. He was Kuichy, the shaman. A full-blooded Inca, Kuichy was very articulate. Well-educated in England, he taught the Inca language and Inca history at the University of Cusco in Peru. After he spoke and everyone else had a moment with him, I approached him. A glass of red wine on the floor between us tipped over, spilling wine on the floor and breaking. Kuichy and I said "Mazel tov" at the same time. We embraced, and he invited me to accompany him to Cusco and attend the Festival of *Qoyllur Rit'i*, an annual weeklong gathering and pilgrimage of the Inca tribes in the mountains. This sounded great; but, I wondered, where would the money come from to pay for this adventure?

The answer came the next day, when Connie asked if I would paint the house, for which she would pay me. So, off to the paint store we went to get all the necessary paint and tools for the job. By the end of the week, I had finished the painting. Pleased with the work, Connie paid me enough to buy a roundtrip plane ticket to Cusco. And off I embarked on this new adventure.

Upon my arrival in Peru, Kuichy greeted me at the airport, and took me to the hotel where I would be staying while in Cusco. We began our adventure right away. Cusco is located in the mountains of Peru, at an elevation of 12,000 feet, and it takes time to become acclimated to the thin air. We visited all of the temples in the surrounding area; then Kuichy brought me to a cave. Telling me to enter, he said that he would meet me at the other end. As I emerged, I saw a sweet little Inca girl, wearing a colorful dress and hat and a necklace, holding a bouquet of wildflowers. Handing the bouquet to me, she then removed and handed me her necklace. The necklace was a representation of the Southern Cross constellation, an Inca symbol. From there, Kuichy and I proceeded to the reflecting pools of water that the Incas had used for stargazing. The Incas would look into these pools, which captured and isolated individual constellations. An interesting way to study a particular constellation in detail.

Returning to town, I hung out at the Mama Africa Café. There was a buzz in the air. We were in a vortex of energy like none I had ever experienced. Sitting on the veranda, I looked out over the center square in Cusco and beyond, gazing upon this reality that had stood the test of time, architectural forms organized in so many layers of expression throughout history. Here lay hidden mystery, mystique, and an infectious passion filling the air and moving through the atmosphere in ways we are unaware, expressing itself in the magic spell it casts upon us.

The Children of the Stars had gathered from distant places to play where the sky and the Earth touch the souls in a gentle rapture. As I walked the cobblestone streets, amidst all the hustle and bustle, however, I could also sense fear. I detected an unwillingness among the tourists to let go of their fears, a distrust, an attachment to personal possessions. But unattachment was the way of this place, of this time; it wasn't about ownership but about trust.

The next day, Kuichy picked me up for our journey to the place where our pilgrimage, the Festival of Qoyllur Rit'i, also called the Quest for Christ, would begin: The village of Mawayani, located in the Valley of Sinakara at the foot of Mount Ausangate, a 20,872-foot-high peak. It took us eight hours of driving on dirt roads, over riverbeds, through villages, and over mountains for us to reach Mawayani.

Arriving, we joined more than 30,000 indigenous people who had gathered in the Valley of Sinakara, surrounded by towering snow-covered peaks. Tribes and families were camped in the valley. Fires, horses, dogs, children playing — the sounds were constant, day and night. Everyone was dressed in traditional costumes, chanting and singing, a colorful sea of people. One legend goes that a man of fair skin and beard had made an appearance, performed miracles, then left an impression of his face on a cloth that a peasant woman had given him to wipe his face. This cloth hangs in the church that had been built on this site.

The pilgrimage was a five-hour hike to reach the Sanctuary of the Snow Star at Qoyllur Rit'i, Mount Ausangate. As I moved along, I found myself in a gridlock of people, and soon realized what "Being One" was all about. I just went with the flow; there was nothing else I could do. There was no turning back; I had to go in the direction of the crowd to the heart of the event. Along the path, incense burned and burning candles dripped wax. Occasionally, fire would flare up from all the candle wax, singeing the hair on my arms. The church bell never stopped ringing. This was the most intense gathering I have ever attended.

As a result of all the incense and candle smoke, I caught a chest cold. Moreover, when everyone came back down to the village and started their vehicles, clouds of suffocating diesel smoke filled the air. All I could breathe was carbon monoxide. All of this brought home to me the clear realization that we must stop using fossil fuels. I advise anyone attending the Festival of Qoyllur Rit'i to either leave the day before, or the day after, the Festival's end in order to avoid the choking vehicle smoke.

CHAPTER THIRTY-EIGHT
AT THE TOP OF THE WORLD

I returned to Cusco just in time to join with 12 other world travelers, about to embark on a Snow Tours trek to Machu Picchu, who were gathered just down the hallway from the Mama Africa Café. A bus picked us up, and then took us to another bus that we boarded for the drive to the Urabamba Valley, where our journey along the Inca trail would begin. The members of our group were Michael Melsinger, of Germany; Hannah Cosh, Sarah Gordon, Andy Giffin, and Heidi Laviers, of the United Kingdom; Gwen Tierres and Andrea Barsony, of France; Monica Arganares, of Argentina; Sam Marino, of Canada; Kirsi Mallera and Janica Anderson, of Finland; and Daniel O'Rourk and me, of the United States.

We were all filled with excitement and enthusiasm for what lay ahead on the Inca trail, like so many other mountaineers who have been enticed by Machu Picchu — its mystical lore, its magnetism, that grips your imagination. I was here to satisfy my mythic and poetic curiosity over the magic that had called me, inspired me, motivated me, to come here.

Crossing over the Urabamba River, we began our hike. Accompanying us were porters and a guide, which made hiking a lot easier. The first leg of the journey was tough, the pace fast because we had to reach our first campsite before dark. Kirsi wasn't feeling well and wanted to quit, but we talked her into waiting to see how she felt after a meal and a good night's rest. At about dusk, we arrived at the campsite, finding that everything had already been set up and dinner prepared. When we were settled, I gave a massage to Kirsi; my skills in this area proving useful in making her feel better.

That first night was beautiful; and, for the first time, I saw the Southern Cross. Fixing my eyes upon this portal, I wondered what other explorers had been guided by this

167

constellation. The Milky Way filled the sky overhead, making it a bit hard to clearly make out the Cross, so I just sat on a rock, gazing at the sky, listening to the sounds of the night. A river was roaring by, and I imagined myself on stage, the stars comprising an audience of ancient ancestors, all of my ancestors back to the beginning of time, shining their light on me. Suddenly a cow appeared on the trail, and we stared at each other for a moment. I could only make out the cow's shadowy silhouette, and its eyes sparkling from the starlight. This brought me back from my star traveling, and I decided to call it a night. However, I couldn't fall asleep; I could only lie there, resting on the earth, until the stars gave way to daylight. Sleep was out of the question, as poor Kirsi was sick all night.

At the crack of dawn I was up, doing some stretching, when a woman dressed in a colorful traditional outfit, carrying a baby on her back, rode past the camp on a horse. The others began to rise, and the porters fixed breakfast. The conversations, as usual, were fascinating, with everyone speaking at least two, if not three, languages fluently — French, Spanish, German, and, for me, English. Kirsi was crying, sick from a headache and an upset stomach, and still wanted to turn back, so I tuned into her by massaging her neck and shoulders. I told her that if she went back we would miss her very much, and that it seemed like destiny had brought all of us together for this journey. The others gathered around her, offering medicine to relieve her pain. One of the porters helped by taking her backpack, and off we hiked into the new day.

We crossed a tree log bridge, passed through a rain forest with a microclimate, proceeded across a landscape filled with flowers, and negotiated lots of rock steps up and over three mountain ranges. Finally, we reached our next campsite, located at an altitude of 12,874 feet. Looking back over the valleys through which we had crossed that day, I took in the views, which were spectacular. After joining the others, who were chattering away at the dinner table, I excused myself and asked

168

everyone for their attention. I told the group, each person individually, that they were unique individuals. I said that we were on a quest for the Holy Grail, that this journey had been pre-encoded in us, and that it was up to each of us to tap into our cellular memories, as we drew closer to Machu Picchu, for the truth to be revealed. I said that all of this was no mystery. In response, they all just looked at me, and then resumed their conversations.

Remembering that I had a surprise for Kirsi, I took one of the water bowls used for hand washing and filled it with water. Removing her shoes, I washed her feet, and then massaged them. She really appreciated this gesture. We started talking, and she told me that she was studying to be a psychologist. I told her that if she completed this journey, she would have the confidence to do anything she put her mind to. After I finished Kirsi's massage, Daniel asked me to massage his shoulders. Then Gwen asked if I would massage her right calf, which had been getting tight and knotted up, causing cramps. I was glad I could be of service to my new friends.

A special synergy suffused our group. I was surprised at how mature and wise the members of this group seemed to be. You meet the most interesting people on great adventures, which is why I like to travel internationally. Although the others were much younger than me, they still possessed a sensitivity for each other, expressed as human grace.

I called our guide "Speedy Gonzales," because he was always walking so fast, trying to keep things moving, in order to get us to camp before dark. He would explain all the vegetation along the trail, my favorite being the purple, white, and yellow Marguerite flowers growing in bunches along the trail. At one point, "Gonzales" drew three circles on the ground, representing three mountains: Mount Ausangate, 20,872 feet tall; Mount Salkantay, 20,574 feet tall; and Mount Veronica, 18,635 feet tall. Connecting the circles with straight lines, he illustrated how these three mountains formed a triangle. Then he drew, in the center of the triangle, a fourth circle, which represented Machu Picchu. His ground picture was a clear illustration of Machu Picchu's location, and why it was so special. Pointing towards the mountains, he said, "Tomorrow we go there."

Finally we reached our last campsite, at Phuyupatamarka, located above Machu Picchu at an altitude of 11,745 feet. At this elevation, we were above the clouds, overlooking the most beautiful view you could imagine. The sun was setting through clouds drifting by, with the snow-covered peaks appearing and vanishing as the clouds changed shape. If heaven is the dimension of one's soul, then I did a dimensional analysis at that moment, standing there at the top of the world. My physical relationship clear, my soul embraced the magnitude of this experience. Everyone was just blown away by the view. That night, my companions and I enjoyed our last supper together as a group, and we celebrated.

During the meal, we pitched in money to tip the porters, and Andrea had the honor of presenting our token of appreciation to them for all they had done for us. The porters had a surprise for us as well — hot wine with lemon, a real treat. Michael had wished for a glass of wine at every meal, and now at last his wish had come true. Sam was always wishing for peanut butter, but unlike the wine this delicacy never materialized. As we sipped on our glasses of hot wine, a sudden silence overcame us all. What a wonderful commitment to will, I thought, a union of spirits brought together to show up and support each other by just being present and participating. As Woody Allen once said, "Ninety percent of success is just showing up."

The next morning we awoke at 3:00 o'clock in order to get an early start for the last leg of the hike, a climb up a steep set of steps leading to the terrace overlooking Machu Picchu. Reaching this vantage point, we were treated to the classic view of Machu Picchu, the image you always see in the picture postcards.

The morning light guiding our way, we hiked down to Machu Picchu, the Crystal City. Reaching the city, the long-anticipated moment having arrived at last, we all yelled, and there was much hand clapping. We were tired, stiff, and sore. But we had all made it, even Kirsi. I was so happy for her that she had hung in there.

What an amazing architectural monument to posterity and preservation Machu Picchu is — a symbol of a civilization, a culture, that had honored and lived in harmony with its environment. Truly the ancient dwellers here had possessed a common-sense love and respect for the beauty all around them, reflected in all directions. Having also developed a great comprehension and awareness of astronomy, they were tuned into the cosmic cycle and stellar phenomena. It is all told in the stories laid out in their architecture, in their ingenious imagination, manifested in their precise craftsmanship and stone-working techniques. Unbelievable.

As we all gathered for a group photo, hummingbirds buzzed around, sucking sweet nectar from the flowers. Suddenly we saw, circling in the sky overhead, a condor, as rainbows appeared all around in the sky. I looked at each member of our group, each one of these precious beings with whom I had shared this experience. I will hold them dear in my heart forever.

Hannah: Always so British-like, her radiance shining brighter and brighter with every step she took, showing her true Aries nature, climbing the summits with grace; she had the charisma of Princes Di. Sarah: A glow in her eyes, the intense sparkling light of the all-knowing Taurus, who seemed to be having a wonderful affair with life. Gwen: So enthusiastic about Machu Picchu; the first to arrive, always present and alert, like the mighty Taurus she is. Monica: With a hidden message tucked away; as soon as she realizes it, she will shoot her arrow with the accuracy of Sagittarius, hitting center. Sam, "I am, Green Eggs and Ham": A teacher in Canada, with the instincts of the awakening puma with Aquarius' wisdom; he will inspire many young minds and feed them peanut butter and jelly sandwiches. Kirsi: Champion Aries, unstoppable, now standing on the threshold of a new psychology, yet to be understood, about inner knowing. Janica: The Pisces Goddess of Nourishment, through her blue aqua soul, radiating love and kindness. Daniel: The Leo, wearing the Crown Chakra of the heavenly star knowledge, holding the key to the Milky Way (chocolate candy bar). Andy: The Cancer, who will invent new technology that will put humanity on the path to unlocking cellular memories. Heidi: Precious Pisces, sitting in silence, observing all; when she smiled, her compassion poured out of every pore of her being. Andrea: Master Virgo, who will create and be editor-in-chief of one of the greatest compilations of wisdom ever electronically published. Michael: Hercules in his past life, able to move illusionary walls with the strength of his mind.

As for me, the Capricorn that I am, I will hold these truths at the zenith of my heart and soul. "So be it," my brothers and sisters of peace and love. This is dedicated to the 12 precious angels who walked with me on the Inca trail to the City of Light.

CHAPTER THIRTY-NINE
MOVING PICTURES

Leaving the top of the world, I returned to Aspen for what would be my final summer there. I would soon be leaving to attend film school in Sedona, Arizona. My passion for film had long possessed me, and the time had come for me to focus on my love of telling stories on film. My time in Aspen had been a very creative period in my life.

A fun film I made in Aspen featured a yoga teacher named Sally Flanagan, a waitress at the Main Street Bakery, who often waited on me at breakfast. One day, as I was sitting in the Zele Café, Sally approached me, saying she would like to perform on film for me, and launched into a dance routine she had choreographed. After watching her, I told her to meet me at the Aspen Museum for an art opening, where I would film her on the stage attached to the back of the Museum. She showed up and I filmed her, thus beginning a creative relationship between us. I often used Sally in my story ideas, one of which was titled, *She is Poetry*. In fact, I almost married Sally so that she could become an American citizen. We discussed it, but then she had to leave the country before we made a commitment.

Another of my films featured Othello, an African-American friend of mine, a snowboarding and skateboarding instructor, who had his own line of designer clothing and a business selling his product line. Othello and I had often talked about doing a short film together about him; then we blocked out some ideas and set a date to shoot. We went out one sunny, snow-covered day, and I followed him and a few of his students around with my camera. The resulting film, *Othello in Aspen*, was shown in the "Local Shorts" category during the Aspen Film Festival.

The year 2002 had been a great year for me. The US Comedy Arts Festival, sponsored by HBO, featured a great week of entertainment and guest speakers; and the HBO Freedom of Speech Award ceremony was really special. I had a front row seat at the Wheeler Opera House, where I watched as George Carlin and Dick Gregory received this honor, preceded by documentary film clips of their careers that introduced them. I appeared on HBO's *Live from Aspen* with Michael Budman, the owner of Roots Clothing Store on Galena Street, in front of the store in my clown persona. Yes, a very special year.

I got together with another friend, Scott Hollander, the son of Gino Hollander, the famous local painter, and filmed an hour-long piece for local *Grassroots TV*, in which I played the main character, riding around Aspen on my bicycle. I took the viewers on a tour of "A day in the life of Hinton Harrison in Aspen," meeting the friends whom I frequently visited during my daily activities. The piece was called, *Cowboy on a Bike.*

I often visited Crestone, Colorado, another of my favorite towns, over in the San Luis Valley along the Sangre de Cristo Mountains. There lived my friend, Rachel Amor, an Apache girl. She was a very interesting, enterprising person, a real "shape shifter," who was involved in lots of different activities. She was also a medicine woman. Inspired by our friendship, I made a film about her called, *Apache Vision.*

It was while visiting Sedona, Arizona, on one of my trips to the southwest, that I had discovered a film school there. Applying to the school, I was accepted in 2002, after pitching my film concept called, *Shadow Being.* Leaving Aspen, I moved to Sedona, and started classes in the film school's narrative program in late August.

My film *Shadow Being* was about a Native American Veteran who returns home to an unfriendly world, unheralded by his country, and is left to his own devices to find himself again.

After completing a rehabilitation program through Veterans Affairs, he sets out on a Vision Quest to reconnect with his ancestral traditions, only to find that his homeland has been desecrated by development. He now turns to the elemental forces of the universe, calling on earth, wind, fire, and water to cleanse him so that he may return home to his source star.

My experience in film school provided me with an interesting lesson; transcendence would be the best word to describe what happened to me. There is something about the movie environment that brings out the strangest aspects of human nature that I have ever experienced in my life. Understanding the human psyche is certainly a mystery that will always remain as complicated as the DNA of each individual. Creativity is greeted with passionate denial and challenged by every insecurity, hampered with obstacles of resistance by every bit of skepticism humanly possible, breeding resentment. School is the most oppressive, most depressing, of environments — an environment in which creativity is suffocated by the bureaucracy of an over-regulated system that is controlled by the government.

So what did I do after completing the first year? I went back to the school for a second year, in the Documentary Program, only to find that the teacher, whom I'd had in the first year, disliked me, judging me negatively as a person. This set a precedent for the attitude of my fellow students towards me for the rest of the year. This attitude translated into animosity, misunderstanding, and unpopularity, even outright slander, directed at me. I might as well have been sitting on a stool, wearing a dunce cap, as I'd done back in elementary school so many years ago. This climate made learning anything from the instructor just about impossible for me. Technically, he was too advanced, and had no patience in teaching someone like me who was computer-illiterate. So it was actually a waste of money for me to go through the program. It was disappointing and frustrating to even go to the school. So I went to Los Angeles, filmed my documentary, mailed it in, then left the school and was glad to be out of the place.

I take full responsibility for my choices. I have made some bad ones in my life; and attending film school was one of them, especially in light of all the abuse I had been subjected to in the past. I was uncomfortable in film school; and, personally, I believe that schools are unhealthy environments. If I had it all to do over again, I wouldn't subject myself to film school. I'd just take the money, buy a camera, read the camera's operating manual, then film my stories and get on with my life.

My documentary short film was titled, *7007 Thousand Sunsets*, about a character, played by me, trying to raise money to make a movie. My character doesn't raise any money, but does succeed in making an 18-minute short that costs only two DVC tapes. In one scene, my character bumps into Britney Spears on the street in Venice Beach, a little clip that was bought by *Access Hollywood*. My cameraperson, David Sereda, had contacted them and sold it to them for $1,500. So, in a way, my film actually did make some money. I consider this film to be a concept piece, a work in progress. A journey to be continued.

Like my main character in the film, I find myself walking on Hollywood Boulevard, all alone in the night. Looking down, I see outstanding stars passing under my feet. What achievements had placed their names on this boulevard? Now I see what I am: A self-luminous being full of creative energy, charged by a distant star in the heavenly sky, finding my way through the atmosphere that will influence my personal destiny. Hollywood beckons me. Yes, that twinkling starlight does attract — the star, the symbol of Hollywood, of Hollywood's glamour, of Hollywood's success. It is no wonder that celebrities are called "STARS."

CHAPTER FORTY
FREEDOM

After leaving film school, I found myself shifting from an introverted artist to an activist faced with challenging questions about freedom of expression. There is something in our institutions that undermines the human spirit. Again, I find myself at a crossroads, broken down emotionally, stuck between freedom and totalitarian authority, trying not to make wrong choices that will drag on forever, for time is too valuable and life is short. Let me express my feelings by using words that others have used to create a picture. You might say I have stolen these words.

We live in such a corrupted, corrupt, society; and if we don't get back on course and return to our original concepts of freedom, we will degenerate into a collectivist society, and then it will be too late to change. Our government officials are becoming rulers instead of servants of the people. The rights of individuals and the rights of society seem to always be in conflict, a global dilemma as "Democracy," which is not synonymous with "Freedom," is spreading around the world. As the mystifying politicians take more and more civil liberties away from the average citizen, and with the high cost living and low wages, it is becoming impossible to make ends meet. The gap between "them that got" and "them that don't got" is widening.

The American lifestyle is all about the sovereignty of individual free choices; and when a government dominates a free society, it erodes personal liberties, and those liberties are soon destroyed. This is the age in which government believes that violating the rights of some individuals is justified in order to secure the interests of political parties and special interest groups. These small, self-centered groups are taking the wealth out of the pockets of citizens and using it to fund their own personal agendas and lifestyles. Taking power from their countrymen.

They use the Constitution as the justification for their moral crusades, talking equality while stealing the rights of the people. The Constitution is all about equality and the right to pursue equal opportunity for all individuals. There are vital questions we must ask of ourselves. Are our lifestyle and desire for material things contributing to the decay of our Constitutional Rights? Does this materialism support a system that interferes with individual freedom? Does anyone have the right to violate the rights of others? Future generations must understand the importance of a free society, the importance of respecting the rights of every man and woman to pursue his or her own liberty and happiness.

Underlying "Of the People, by the people, and for the people" is the spirit of a freethinking people who will never submit to, or live under, totalitarian government rule. Be aware that just because someone is in favor of "Freedom" doesn't mean that they respect YOUR freedom. What freedom is to one person could be devastating to the freedom of another. Liberty, to me, means doing what I want to do with my life. To someone else, liberty might mean doing whatever he or she wants to do with MY life, with YOUR life. The definition of freedom is, "Being free, not under the control or power of another."

Nature has rendered freedom and equality incompatible. To bring about equality, force is often used. Therefore, someone is under the control or power of another, so freedom exits. Often, when people scream "Freedom!" they really mean their own concept of freedom; and in gaining their freedom, they violate your freedom. It is the same with peace: Fighting a war for peace is a strange concept.

Freedom means that everyone is "free," but a pure state of freedom is foreign and difficult to understand, because people need rules. Nature is cruel, and because of the reality of man's nature, freedom must be restricted. You give a man absolute freedom, and the result will be total chaos. So now the question is this: Whose freedom, if anyone's, needs to be restricted, and to what extent, if any, does it need to be restricted in order to "protect freedom"?

We live in a complex society; and often, to those who cannot achieve success in a free world come jealousy, a worthless human emotion. Jealous people would rather force everyone to conform to their moral ways than appreciate the success of others, thereby imposing their definition of freedom on the targets of their jealousy.

Freedom is a word used only for convenience these days. Look at our present situation in the Middle East: What is our vested interest, and whose freedom are we fighting for, when we force our way of life on others? It all seems to start with our parents and teachers, who influence us with their beliefs, and with the government, which is supposed to be the collective representation of the hearts and minds of a society of free people.

Although we have the Constitutional right to pursue happiness, it is difficult to convince me that we have the right to be "happy."

I keep to my own counsel, taking into consideration the negative side of things. This allows me to formulate a way out, an escape route, something ingrained in me during my military training. One positive aspect of my time in the service. I do not mean to discourage anyone, but, rather, to root out any impediments for greater success in achieving all of the wonderful things that life has to offer. I desire nothing more than to be free to enjoy life. My lifestyle might terrify an ordinary person. I take risks, I break with existing authority, I am quick and willing to change at any moment, and I am not attached to anything that would make me possessive of anything other than my own civil liberties.

So here I am now, living in North Hollywood, California, in the Valley of the Stars, putting pen to paper. Out of my imagination pops abstract concepts. I sit here thinking, reasoning, categorizing, and writing; and it is my hope that, in reading this book, my words will project inspiring pictures into your mind. I think that the human brain is a microcosmos, and that each of us is a planetarium of elemental stardust atoms produced by an exploding star. Each of us surfing the expanse of space itself, each of us an extraterrestrial being in sympathetic harmony with the essence of its genius.

What keeps me going is painting myself out of my most recent depression, going into that place to which I retreated as a child to escape violence. Now painting, now writing, now telling stories on film, I am brought back into the present. Now clearing the slate and starting over, I wonder what influence Los Angeles will have on me. Writing this book has been a cathartic experience for me. Looking at my life, I ask myself: What is my story telling me? The answer is, it is telling me to keep it simple, to keep moving forward, and to not look back.

CHAPTER FORTY-ONE
CHASING DESTINY

Again, I find myself chasing destiny, leaping into the unknown, looking for meaning in my life, trying to create something out of nothing, seeking a challenge to pursue. Riding on the rippling wave of adventure, trusting in luck, searching until I find what I am looking for, and unleashing my human potential, the engine of prosperity. Los Angeles is a quivering vortex of super-gravitational power. To describe it would be like explaining the black hole theory: You get sucked into this mass concentration of talent, and there is no way to escape this swirling pool of space-time creativity that you clasp onto. You can only hope to come out the other side a better person, a better star-being. I must become inwardly free, the master of my own destiny, for truly there is no tyranny as enslaving as my own emotions. I must take control of my life, I must set myself free, for my greatest struggle is to stop struggling. In the words of Albert Einstein:

> I am truly a "lone traveler" and have never belonged to my country, my home, my friends, or even my immediate family, with my whole heart; in the face of all these ties, I have never lost a sense of distance and a need for solitude — feelings, which increase with years.

PEACE!

Why can't we all just worship, "Thou shalt not kill"?